THE PUREST
DEMOCRACY
IN THE WORLD

THE PUREST
DEMOCRACY
IN THE WORLD

Avraham C. Ben-Yosef

Herzl Press
and
New York   *Thomas Yoseloff*   *London*

To My Mother

Foreword

I am a rank-and-file member of a kibbutz in Israel. It seems to me that the world in general and the Jews in particular still know far too little about this significant and exciting thing called kibbutz. The present book is composed of a general description of this remarkable sociological phenomenon of our time, together with my first-year diary as a participant in it. Together, I hope, they will convey some idea of the unique local atmosphere of the kibbutz, and perhaps even lead to a personal interest in the subsequent development of this new-old way of life in the new-old Land of Israel.

This book is appearing only a short time after the jubilee celebrations of Kibbutz Degania, the first of them all. Although rather late, I should like to make my own little salute to Degania, the Mother of the Kibbutzim, in honor of her fiftieth birthday, and to acknowledge the fact that her name is an inspiration to all of us in the kibbutz movement.

Among the founding members, not only of Degania, but of the entire kibbutz movement, is Miriam Baratz, who can justifiably be called mother of the Mother of the Kibbutzim. She was treasurer of a tiny experimental commune of workers at Hadera on the Coast Plain even before the move to Degania, on the southern shore of the Sea of Galilee, was made and permanent settlement achieved there on a communal basis. I am greatly privileged to have been favored with a message from her which makes the best possible introduction to the present book. Incidentally, a book on Degania, entitled *A Village by the Jordan* by Joseph Baratz, her husband, is invaluable as a history of the kibbutz movement.

It will be noted that the word "kvutza" is used in Miriam Baratz's message instead of "kibbutz," of which it is virtually the diminutive. In the kvutza, apart from being smaller, there is a feeling of close, intimate, sheer comradeship, which is sometimes lacking in its bigger brother, the highly developed kibbutz of our own day. It is this intensely human aspect which Miriam Baratz wishes to stress when she and her cofounders still use the word kvutza. To be correct, one should therefore speak of Degania as the "Mother of the Kvutzot," her quasi-official, affectionate epithet; only to avoid confusion is the modern form, kibbutz, used throughout this book.

And these are the simple, touching and convincing words (in English translation) of Miriam Baratz who has been a kibbutz member for over fifty years:

"I am a member of a kvutza, in which I grew up and was trained, and from which I received much more than I ever gave to her. I am happy to have witnessed Degania's jubilee, and am proud of her achievements and those of all the kibbutz movement, although I am also aware that there are many difficult problems still ahead of us. I wish all of us a strong and sincere faith in the justice of our way."   AVRAHAM C. BEN-YOSEF

Acknowledgments

In the first place, my sincerest thanks are due to Mr. Avraham Schenker of the Jewish Agency, New York, without whose practical assistance it is unlikely that this book would have materialized at all, and to the editor of the Herzl Press, Dr. Raphael Patai, without whose invaluable supervision it would certainly not have attained presentable form.

I am also greatly indebted to the Audit Union of the Workers' Agricultural Cooperative Societies, Ltd., Tel Aviv, whose wide range of advice and help was quite indispensable; and to Dr. H. Darin-Drabkin, Economic Adviser of the Housing Division of the Ministry of Labor, Tel Aviv, who kindly permitted me to use figures from his recent book, *The Other Society* (sifriyat, Hapoalim, Merhavia, Israel 1961). All the statistics quoted regarding kibbutz agriculture and industry, as well as some others, come from this source, which contains a full economic and social survey of the kibbutz, and the most complete kibbutz bibliography extant.

I also wish to thank the Land Settlement Department of the Jewish Agency, Jerusalem; the Central Office of Statistics, Tel Aviv; the management of "The Family of the Kibbutz" Exhibition, Tel Aviv, 1961; the Ihud Hakvutzot Vehakibbutzim; Hakibbutz Hameuhad; Hakibbutz Haartzi; and Messrs. Faber & Faber, Ltd., of London, publishers, for their kind permission to quote a paragraph from C. E. M. Joad's *Guide to Modern Wickedness.*

Finally, I should like to express my gratitude to my fellow kibbutz members, Yitzhak Krul and Avi Shahar, who helped me on the spot, where we live on our 3,000-foot-high Galilean mountaintop—Kibbutz Sasa, the highest kibbutz in the land!   AVRAHAM C. BEN-YOSEF

A Note to the Reader

This is, in a way, an unusual book. It is not usual to combine a theoretical description and an immigrant's diary, as has been done here. But there is a purpose in it —the one is intended to illustrate the other, for the subject matter itself is unusual—which is to say, far too little known, in view of its significance. And finally there is something unusual about this note to you, for it is none other than an invitation to contact the author directly and raise your questions personally with him, in case you want to know more about a point or an issue not covered in the book in sufficient detail. Or, if you plan to arrange a kibbutz holiday in Israel, now or later, summer or winter (you pay for your keep by suitable light work, but you do have to pay your own fare, as the scanty funds available are reserved for our persecuted brothers), write to: Avraham C. Ben-Yosef, Kibbutz Sasa, Doar Na, Merom Hagalil, Israel. Through individual contact in this way, it may be possible to introduce you to the kibbutz and enrich your life by participation in this purest democracy in the world.

Contents

Illustrations

The following illustrations appear as a group following page 126.

BOOK I

The Purest Democracy in the World

I

Democracy and the Kibbutz

It is difficult to write about democracy nowadays. Too many ghosts hover around the typewriter, from Pericles to John Stuart Mill, and beyond in both directions in time. Only a writer of superlative social understanding dare tackle the subject with any hope of making a useful contribution.

No such enterprise is contemplated here. All that is intended is to point up one particular, and still relatively neglected, aspect of democracy in action. Incidentally, some light may be thrown on the spirit of democracy in general, but if so, no pretense is made to it being anything but incidental.

Democracy, as we know it only too well in our time, is a curiously vague concept, so richly set in a mass of associations that when we attempt a definition devoid of such associations it slips out of our hands altogether. There is hardly another concept more precious to us; yet it is extremely difficult to give a specific definition of it. This is not a unique situation, but rather indicates that what the term really stands for is an attitude, an atmosphere, rather than a narrowly definable institution.

In ancient Greece, democracy meant the rule of the majority as opposed to that of some minority or a single and absolute monarch. In modern times, the term has become idealized to imply the rule of all the people by themselves. In practice, to say that the ideal has been but imperfectly realized is to put matters mildly indeed. During most of history, the concept of democracy either remained theoretical or was forgotten altogether. Only comparatively recently, with the rise of capitalism, have various forms of class rule developed out of feudal bases, and led to numerous types of representative government which constitute the different kinds of political democracy known to us today.

It is possible to argue indefinitely with most people as to how far equality is of the essence of democracy, how far and in what form democracy calls for leadership by individuals or groups, and how class domination can best be eliminated so that democracy really amounts to rule "of the people, by the people, for the people." These problems can appropriately be dealt with only in treatises examining the sources of social action on a psychological basis, and that is far removed from the present purpose. But some light can surely be thrown on all these matters by an examination of the broadest, if not the deepest, manifestation of community living found within the realm of modern Western culture, and to this end the present pages are devoted.

In a sense, it is possible to say that no system of representative government is really democratic. Once the limits of direct democracy—self-government by all the people in general meeting—are passed, as of course they must be in all but small communities, something different from the original concept arises. Interest, therefore, persists in the original Athenian model itself. Without going into all

the details of Athenian political organization, two fundamental points may be selected as immediately relevant.
First, the entire citizenry was enfranchised and could participate in the frequent meetings of the Assembly; and,
second, the councilors and some other officials were
elected annually. It is true that women, slaves, and foreign residents were not counted as citizens; and that, on
occasion, re-election took place to a considerable extent;
but the basic principles were firm. The spirit in which
they were applied is well shown in Pericles' remark, "We
are unique in regarding men who take no part in politics
as not merely unambitious but unprofitable; and we are
all sound judges, if not creative statesmen, in public
affairs." There is something peculiarly magnificent in this
remark. It shows that Greek democracy at its finest was not
the rather slack, taken-for-granted kind we know all too
well today. Although only a small proportion of the "citizens" usually attended any one meeting of the Assembly,
there can be no doubt that politics was always in the air,
that democracy was alive, and that public affairs were regarded by most people as an integral part of their own
lives. We know that this kind of direct democracy had its
imperfections, such as the misleading of the public by
demagogues, the irresponsible use of power, and so on. But
it nevertheless worked, in the sense that there was a community spirit alive in the populace. It was not a case of the
people standing apart and leading their daily individual
lives, while the government functioned as an impersonal
entity in the background, with a modicum of contact between the two on election days only. With all its limitations, democracy in ancient Greece was a reality the like of
which has hardly ever been achieved since; except, that
is, in small-size cooperative communities.

Our interest, consequently, jumps directly to these co-operative communities, and mainly to the most outstandingly successful variety of them that has as yet arisen—the modern Israeli *kibbutz*. But, even if only in passing, a word about representative government in general seems in order. For democracy in our time has come to mean representative government; the huge population aggregates of modern states make direct self-government through a unitary assembly impracticable. No return, therefore, to the Greek type of direct democracy is possible, and no proposal leading in that direction will be put forward. All that is suggested is that an examination of current Israeli small-scale direct democracy is worth the effort because it can bring us as near to the original reality of living democracy practiced by the ancient Greeks as we can reasonably hope to come. This is a worthwhile venture which may open up possibilities for the revitalizing of our democracy.

It is generally accepted that the purpose of any representative governmental system is to enable the individual people to give expression to their personal wishes and to shape the government accordingly. A truly representative government, therefore, far from being a remote impersonal entity, is precisely its opposite. The trouble is that the larger the society or the state, the more difficult it is for the individual citizen to exert direct influence on his government, or to participate actively in its conduct of affairs. It is, of course, impossible for the ordinary citizen nowadays to vote on questions of foreign, or indeed any major domestic, policy; he must leave such matters to his representative. But he can participate in local government, and in any good representative system he must have the power to bypass his representative if he feels this to be necessary, and to make direct application to the highest competent government official. Nothing seems more regrettable in most modern democracies than the fact—often admitted —that local government is largely moribund. Thus, on the local level, too, democracy frequently has little if any practical meaning. This is inevitable if the ordinary man does not engage in at least some form of public political service. To become a member of a political party—even an active member—is hardly sufficient in itself, although it is an important step in the right direction. The ideal must be public service, and this precisely is the keynote of the kibbutz, the apex of modern Israeli democracy, which we propose to examine.

The other basic principle of ancient Greek democracy, the insistence on frequent change of officials, aimed at preventing the establishment of a permanently entrenched bureaucracy. As some students of the subject have pointed out recently, a certain amount of bureaucracy is not a bad thing; only in excess does officialdom become a nuisance instead of fulfilling public functions efficiently. Permanent clerks in the civil service of a country are, of course, no menace, not even if they occupy senior or top positions; it is the representatives of the people who fill the highest ranks on the policy-making levels who should be recallable frequently and should certainly not be reappointable more than a few times. Otherwise, there is the danger that they might forget that they are merely the representatives and, therefore, the servants of the public, and accordingly try, and probably succeed, to rule the people instead of acting on their behalf. The question of how far the people's wishes can be or should be heeded by their leaders is *the* problem of democratic leadership.

The kibbutz has squarely faced up to these dangers and

problems. Its officials are, in general, changed annually, except in the case of those who have a great deal to learn before they can do their jobs properly; the latter are allowed to continue in their positions for two or three years.

It is generally considered that frequent elections interfere too much with the ordinary life of the citizens. It would, however, be logical to contend that such interference was a good thing in itself and, within reason, should not be opposed. One may argue that most modern democracies have rendered their government less truly representative than it might have been by spacing their elections so far apart that the ordinary citizen regards them as extraordinary, rare events which have hardly any bearing on his personal life. It seems a pity, too, that the referendum has, as a rule, been eliminated from the political life of democratic countries. More frequent opportunities to express its views directly would undoubtedly increase the interest of the citizenry in governmental institutions. Change of officials in a direct democracy is, of course, not the same thing as change of representatives in a representative democracy; but the two are related in that the aim in both cases is to prevent the democracy from becoming a static structure.

And so to the kibbutz itself. "Kibbutz" is Hebrew for "group." In practice the word has come to mean a group of people living and working a collective farm together. An urban kibbutz is not an impossibility and has even been tried, unsuccessfully: this matter will be dealt with later. The feminine form of the word is "kvutza," and is used to designate a small group. In the days when kibbutzim were small and comprised no more than a few dozen people, they were frequently called kvutzot. Nowadays, there are comparatively few kvutzot remaining: they have long since grown too big and consequently consider themselves kibbutzim. As a matter of fact, a group of people who pool their earnings during the preliminary phase of building up a kibbutz community, even though they are still working in private jobs or constitute an organized group on a training farm, consider and call themselves a kibbutz.

So much for the name and its general meaning and usage. Before entering into a description of what is involved, it is perhaps worthwhile to mention very briefly that community living in the Western world has been fundamentally connected with religion. The early Jewish Essenes and, following them, the early Christians formed themselves into such communities, pooling their incomes—or rather their voluntary poverty. The monasteries and convents which came to play an increasingly important role in the religious life of subsequent centuries, were, to all intents and purposes, religious kibbutzim, although, of course, with the sexes separated and no family life. In many parts of Europe during the Middle Ages, small groups of devout Christians lived in community, outside the framework of the monasteries, engaging jointly in missionary activities; the followers of St. Francis of Assisi are to be counted among these. A specially interesting case is that of those Anabaptists who became known as the Hutterite Brethren in Moravia and other parts of Central Europe. To their present-day spiritual heirs further reference will be made, for they form probably the most important group of communalists in the modern world outside the kibbutzim themselves.

Approaching modern times, the well-known reaction of Robert Owen to the social horrors of the Industrial Revolution resulted in his experimental formation of excellent forerunners of kibbutzim. They all failed, it is true, in both

Britain and in America, breaking up under the stress of individualist noncooperation, presumably because Owen accepted all and sundry without verifying their suitability, and his "kibbutzim" thus contained numerous uncooperative individuals who could not be welded into a cohesive community. The question of whom to accept and whom to exclude is to this day a vexing one for the kibbutz, and will have to be dealt with at some length later. In America in particular, experiments in living in kibbutz-like communities have been continually tried by small, specialized groups, sometimes of no more than a few families, sometimes of many hundreds of persons. A study of their history is of great sociological interest. A few examples, such as the Shakers, a religious sect, are fairly well known. Several small communities of this type still exist in the United States and in Canada.

Of these, the history of the Hutterites is unusually interesting. They are known as Primitive Christians, owing to their determination to return to the original tenets of Christianity, which they interpret in a pacifist sense. Because of their refusal to take part in national politics, let alone war, they have been driven from country to country through the centuries. Many thousands emigrated first eastwards to Russia and afterwards westwards to Canada. Their first cooperative community involving community of goods was founded in 1529. In 1920, an inspired German, quite independent of the four-century-old Hutterite movement, founded a community based on similar principles of pure Christianity. This *Bruderhof,* or "brothers' court," of Eberhard Arnold, began with a handful of disciples, grew to moderate dimensions in Germany, was forced to leave that country when Hitler came to power, moved to England via Liechtenstein, and, owing to British restrictions during World War II, migrated to Paraguay. A few members left behind in England, however, succeeded in developing a small but well-established community in the hills on the Welsh border. In recent years, branch communal farms with associated small-scale industrial activities have been opened in Uruguay and the United States, and some were re-established in Germany. The total population of these Bruderhofs is around 5,000 which is quite small compared with the 80,000 of the Israeli kibbutzim, but because of its energetic and pure "kibbutzism" it is especially deserving of notice. An actual merger with the old Hutterite movement has never been effected, and contacts are, in fact, not very intensive; but so close are the ideals of the two groups that, by mutual agreement, they share the name of the great Church leader of the Middle Ages in Central Europe, Jakob Hutter.

From this small modern branch movement of the Hutterite Brethren, one or two very significant lessons can be learned in connection with "kibbutzism," or the idea of complete communal living in general. The spirit of the Bruderhof is basically different from that of the Israeli kibbutzim, including the religious ones. The Brothers believe that pure Christianity demands nothing less than pure community or absolute brotherhood like that of the Apostles, or the followers of St. Francis. For the Jewish religious kibbutz the communality of the kibbutz is justified in itself, and religion is religion and very orthodox at that; the two fit very well together if required, but it is not claimed that true Judaism demands the kibbutz. The distinction becomes still clearer when one considers that kibbutz democracy is normal democracy in that it rests on majority decisions, whereas Bruderhof democracy is something of a superdemocracy, in which communal matters are discussed until unanimity is reached. This is very similar to the "sense of the meeting" which the Quakers habitually strive for and attain in their deliberations, and is definitely related to it. It presumably takes a longer time than the kibbutz is prepared to devote to its meetings, chronically overlong as they are in any case. The kibbutzim, too, are closely knit ideological communities, as shown by their effective stability, but they make no attempt to be as tightly organized as would be necessary to achieve consistently unanimous decisions. At kibbutz meetings strong opposition may be voiced and maintained; however, loyalty to the kibbutz as a whole ensures acceptance of the majority decision by its opponents, even if occasionally with quite some disgruntlement. Viewed from the perspective of the kibbutz, the superdemocracy of the Bruderhof, with its insistence on complete unanimity, does not seem to be essential for communal living, at any rate not until the art and science of community living is advanced considerably beyond its present stage.

While the driving force of the Hutterite movement— religious communality—is patently clear, it is difficult to throw light on the driving force of kibbutz democracy. It is hardly a love of pure democracy for its own sake, as in ancient Greece. In its origins, the driving force of the kibbutz seems to have been a natural growth rooted in Zionism and in whichever political tendency was favored by the founders. Later it manifested itself in devotion to the kibbutz and its fellow members; in other words, simple, direct, and strong communality. Man is a social animal; one cannot put a group of people together to live their lives entirely in common without something happening to them. What happens is just this phenomenon of community of spirit. But this in itself is certainly insufficient, for, as we know, all too many groups have disintegrated in the past. In the case of the kibbutz movement such disintegration has been almost unknown, for there was something much greater than the kibbutz itself which bound the members together—their responsibility as Zionists to rebuild the ancient Land of Israel. Devotion to political ideals, too, has been a great binding force. To betray the Cause, to betray the Party, was and is unthinkable—with only the very rarest personal exceptions. Sheer loyalty seems to be the root of the matter: loyalty to the Zionist movement, to fellow members, to the federation to which the kibbutz belongs and to its political party; loyalty to the land, the farm, the kibbutz society—and with it the unshakable faith in the Land of Israel as the home of great social ideals which the kibbutz itself daily helps to realize. The net effect of all this is not much less than the religious driving force of the Bruderhof, with which, in fact, the kibbutz has certain psychological attributes in common. Both are characterized by devotion to a cause and an inclusive outlook on life quite distinct from the loose but self-centered viewpoint of the individualist. But unlike that of the Bruderhof, the driving force of the kibbutz is not easy to describe in words; it is not a single thing, and it comprises various influences which are neither simple to analyze nor identical or uniform in all cases. Of the solidity and depth of this driving force, however, there can be no doubt. That it could be strengthened here and there, even today, need not be denied; but that "kibbutzism" is an unshakable factor in Israeli society is more than ever true, and it testifies to the strength of this driving force which is so difficult to explain accurately.

Why and how did the kibbutzim start? The fact is that the first Israeli kibbutzim were not founded for any idealistic reason at all. They were founded because the local conditions were so difficult that there was no hope for individual farming. The workers on the first one or two company farms rebelled against their managers, and decided either to run the place on their own, or not at all. This is what happened at Degania, on the southern shore of the Sea of Galilee, in 1909; and this is how it came about that Kibbutz Degania, now affectionately known as "The Mother of the Kibbutzim," was founded. Since then, Kibbutz Degania has grown bigger than its founders thought was desirable for completely friendly cooperative living; and, in 1920, Kibbutz Degania B was established, a little farther back from the lake. To date, more than two hundred kibbutzim have been added in all parts of Israel, from Galilee to the Negev, dedicated pioneering villages everywhere, but especially along the borders where the closely knit character of the kibbutz type of settlement made it ideal for defense purposes.

In the early days, young mothers could not be spared from work in the field or the farmyard, and consequently children's houses were built and staffed by a *few* women who could care for *all* the kibbutz children—a basic social innovation which will be described in detail later. A more or less standard layout became inevitable for the kibbutz village, however it varied in detail in each particular case according to the terrain: the residential blocks of rooms in a group, usually in rows, but sometimes more artistically arranged; the children's houses in the middle, for maximum security; the farm buildings and animals in another group, separated by a main internal roadway (which became, where possible, an avenue of trees) from the residential area, to which were added lawns, gardens, and trees as opportunity permitted. The communal buildings of the kibbutz (above all the dining hall, which in most cases still doubles as the village hall for all large meetings) were placed as centrally as possible, so as to be easily accessible to all; the showerhouse and laundry were sometimes tucked away into odd corners, but had to be close together to share the hot water from a common boiler. Internal pathways and roadways, and a barbed-wire fence around to keep out marauders, were the other main items necessary to complete the general picture. Access from the nearest main road, whether adjacent or a few miles down a winding track, led through a gateway, guarded at night. Other gateways gave access to the fields and orchards surrounding the village. Improvements have, of course, been steadily made in all kibbutzim, as well as enlargements. The first tents and shacks have given way to well-built stone or concrete houses, the first of which have traditionally been the children's houses and the cowhouse. Muddy paths have given way to well-laid stone walks. Libraries, music rooms, and reading rooms, often grouped in a pleasantly designed building known as a "house of culture," have been built. Tree planting to provide shade has been going on, and lawns and gardens have been added round the houses and public buildings. In certain centrally located kibbutzim secondary schools, serving a neighboring group of kibbutzim, have been erected. In several cases, bequests have enabled the kibbutz to build excellent small museums. An old, well-established kibbutz, first settled some twenty-five or thirty years ago, is indeed a place of beauty today; a young kibbutz may still look rather reminiscent of the encampment that it, like its older sisters in their time, once was; but its members are determined to go the way of the others and achieve a setting of grace and comfort as soon as funds permit.

With all this, a kibbutz is very different in appearance from the private villages (*moshavot*) or the cooperative ones (*moshavim*) of Israel itself, let alone villages in other parts of the world. European villages are usually situated along main roads, with houses and subsidiary buildings built alongside secondary roads as well; the kibbutz is more like a private farm estate, separated from the highway system of the country. It is quite definitely a self-contained entity, and, obviously, looks the social unit it is, quite different from the ordinary individualist village. Its form has been dictated by practical needs of a different order from those prevailing in the traditional villages.

Apart from the Arab minority of about 200,000, most of whom are rural, Israel had, in 1961, a rural population of some 300,000, about one-quarter of whom lived in kibbutzim. The kibbutz population, in 1961, amounted to only about 5 per cent of the total Jewish population of Israel; as in all westernized countries, most people live in towns. There can be no doubt at all that the influence of the kibbutzim on Israeli society as a whole is much greater than their numbers would suggest. This influence is felt especially in the agricultural, cultural, and political fields. The first and second of these can be fairly easily explained; the third is a more specific and significant matter which brings us straight back to that Periclean political vitality which characterizes the purest of democracies.

In agriculture, the gathering of the best available farming manpower and its concerted utilization was obviously the key to the kibbutz's success. The small farmer could hardly hope to compete with it, except perhaps in certain small-scale activities such as chicken farming and market gardening. In such branches as banana growing the kibbutzim have few competitors. In fish breeding they have achieved such outstanding results that they were asked to send one of their experts, under United Nations auspices, to Tahiti, to teach the Tahitians how to raise carp in ponds. The kibbutzim have not become very prominent in the vital Israeli citrus-growing industry, which has been, since the early days, in the hands of company and private owners; but they form the backbone of the Israeli sheep-breeders' association, play important roles in most of the other technical agricultural associations, supply numerous experts to official organizations, and are foremost in developing new strains of forage plants, bringing new land areas under grain cultivation, and introducing such new industrial crops as cotton. The kibbutz farmer can obtain time off for attendance at first-class technical courses while his fellow members substitute for him at home—an arrangement impossible for the individualist farmer, except in the most fortunate circumstances. The kibbutz member has continuous access to sources of technical help considerably in excess of those available to most individual small holders; in addition to which, the kibbutz can afford all manner of machinery and water-supply installations which even a well-organized cooperative village can but rarely attain.

The surprising part about all this is that the kibbutzim are not composed of the children of generations of farmers; they come, for the most part, from ghetto communities of small peddlers, from the offices, banks, and shops of the Western world. The Middle Eastern Jewish immigrants, who had, in some cases, been brought up in an agricultural environment, have not, with rare exceptions, taken to kibbutz living; they have gone in for small holdings more or less cooperative, but have almost never joined or founded kibbutzim, for their entire outlook is quite contrary to the kibbutz spirit. The kibbutz farmer usually had to learn from scratch, gathering what knowledge he could from occasional limited periods in training farms. He also learned much about local agricultural conditions from the Arabs, and more from experience and innumerable initial failures—the hard way, but perhaps not the least valuable of all. His Zionist idealism triumphed over all the difficulties, and his children are now growing up with the beginnings of an agricultural tradition behind them, to which they steadily add strength.

It is a very extraordinary thing that, as has often been admitted, the roots of culture in Israel seem to be rather in the country than in the towns. It is true that the towns —that is to say, the three main cities, Tel Aviv, Haifa, and Jerusalem—are where most concerts, theater performances, and art exhibitions take place; but, in order to meet the rural demand, the orchestras, theater groups, and exhibitions must constantly travel and make the rounds of the villages; and "villages," in this case, mainly mean the kibbutzim, for they have the greatest resources in time, money, and cultural background. In addition to this, the kibbutzim contain notable resources of talent of their own. In a word, cultural life in the kibbutzim is, for the most part, very intensive, ranging from chamber and orchestral music, phonograph concerts, and even amateur opera, to art and other exhibitions, dramatic and dance performances. All these, plus certain festival performances which draw large crowds from the towns into relatively remote rural locations, are important factors in the cultural life of the country as a whole. In the kibbutz, moreover, there is an atmosphere of living participation which is lacking in the mass entertainment of the towns. When the Israel Philharmonic Orchestra plays in Tel Aviv, the occasion is, to a large degree, impersonal; when it visits a kibbutz amphitheater, personal participation of everyone can be sensed immediately in the intimacy of the atmosphere. Incidentally, the concerts of the United Kibbutz Orchestra are often broadcast nationally, and kibbutz art exhibitions are often to be seen in the urban art galleries.

Finally, the obvious question arises, "Why do the kibbutzim have to meddle so much in politics?" It is often considered that the intense political activity of the kibbutzim is undesirable, that it wastes energies better devoted to the other ends, that it splits the kibbutz movement unnecessarily, that it distorts and largely spoils what would otherwise be pure "kibbutzism."

Such a view shows a complete misunderstanding of the situation. Apart from a few exceptional cases, politics is an essential part of kibbutz life. In many kibbutzim, politics takes the place of the weather as the topic of general, casual, everyday conversation. Surprising as this may seem to most people, it is, in fact, quite natural; it logically follows from the fact that "kibbutzism" as a way of life is essentially political to the highest degree. The kibbutz is a form of society based on pure democracy, and, as Pericles pointed out, pure democracy is inconceivable unless everyone participates to some extent in framing its policies. In other words, in that context it would be disgraceful not to be politically minded. An active kibbutz democrat cannot be unmindful of the political society around him, outside the kibbutz, and, indeed, in the world as a whole, for is not his own small community the natural spearhead of the drive towards the ideal world democracy of the future? The few orthodox-religious and independent kibbutzim may have a different outlook of their own, which may not tally with this view; but their very separatism obliges them to search for new political forms of their own. However, a basic and important common characteristic of all kibbutzim is their keen interest in politics.

As a matter of fact, the Jewish people as a whole, and not only that small section of it which lives in kibbutzim, has a penchant for politics. Perhaps the reason is that they were forced into politics by the hard facts of history, just as they were pushed into finance by not being permitted to hold land or to engage in trade. The Zionist movement was organized politically from the outset, and, the Jews having been a people without a land, it had to find a nongovernmental background for its politics. The British Mandatory period provided the political nursery for the Yishuv. By the time of the British evacuation of Palestine, the "shadow government" of the Jewish Agency in Jerusalem was able to transform itself into the Provisional Government of Israel at a moment's notice. These antecedents determined the political character of Israel. It is true, of course, that there are politics and politics, and not all the wrangling has been useful. But, at least, it has had the great merit of keeping the population politically conscious, and thereby keeping alive the ideal of practical democracy. In spite of the splinter parties and inevitable coalitions stemming from proportional representation, and in spite of the inexperience of a young democracy in parliamentary methods and the large percentage of uneducated elements in the welter of its unintegrated population, Israeli parliamentary democracy has proved reasonably stable and satisfactory. Although Israeli politics creates a rather turbulent impression, it works rather well in practice, suggesting that those responsible are not without a flair for balanced political management—as delicate an art as any in the world and one of the most useful.

In such a setting, the kibbutz movement would have been out of place had it not been politically minded from the outset; this, quite apart from the fact that "kibbutzism" logically demands a high level of political consciousness. In any event, the kibbutzim took to politics with burning enthusiasm, and the flame has never dimmed, nor is it in the least likely to do so. Not every kibbutz member need, of course, take an active part in politics, and many actually do not, apart from the minimum of voting; but the way is wide open for all who wish to do so, and they receive every encouragement.

Each of the three main kibbutz federations supports its own political party and has its own national daily newspaper, freely available to all members on the basis of collective and compulsory kibbutz subscriptions. In two of the three federations, the kibbutzim tend to form the backbone of their parties, whose strength is not nearly so pronounced in the towns. This is yet another interesting example of the way in which general social trends are occasionally reversed in Israel. However, kibbutz members do not keep their politics to themselves; they go out into the neighboring towns and villages, spreading their party gospel and, whenever possible, their own kibbutz gospel as well.

The three main federations range from Left to Center, while the small religious federation may be regarded as somewhat closer to the Right. Actually it is necessary to separate in his mind the politics of the kibbutz itself—that is, its philosophy in action—from the politics of the political party to which the kibbutz is affiliated; for kibbutz politics amounts to a pure, fixed, and completely democratic cooperative attitude, whereas party politics, while of necessity militant, seeking either to change the existing order of society or to retain it in the *status quo,* always implies a degree of compromise.

As a way of life, "kibbutzism" is quite capable of standing by itself, even in a noncooperative world; but its inner logic also drives it outwards, not merely to expand as much as possible, but to help make society in general more cooperative, to give itself thereby a more congenial environment, and to encourage people to build a happier, because more mutualistic, society.

It is not infrequently claimed that the kibbutz movement would be both stronger and healthier if it set its internal political differences aside and became completely united. Certain experiences derived from attempts at greater consolidation in other sectors of the Israeli political world would suggest exactly the opposite: internal disputes are likely to arise and serious weaknesses develop as a result of such unification. Certainly, the highest practicable degree of consolidation is desirable, but more harm than good could be done in pressing matters beyond the really feasible stage before the time is ripe. Personal politics lies very close to man's heart. It is better that friends of a like mind should dwell together, and that groupings of differing political complexion should not be forced to live under one roof. There can be no doubt that future opportunities for a higher degree of unification will be taken up enthusiastically as they occur.

Meanwhile, there are many fields apart from politics in which the kibbutz movement already stands solidly united: in agriculture, in art, in attitude to governmental economic policy, there is wholehearted cooperation. Joint projects are being developed and conferences arranged from which the nonkibbutz villages are not excluded. With all its interesting and rich diversity, the kibbutz world is one. Indeed, although more vaguely and loosely, all the Israeli workers' settlements stand together to provide the solid agricultural backbone of the country. A kibbutz is in no way cut off from the rest of society; on the contrary, it cooperates actively with its neighbors of whatever composition, in regional rural councils, and participates to the utmost in the national life of the country.

2

The Organization of the Kibbutz

Kibbutz democracy is far from being a haphazard affair. Although the general meeting of members, usually held weekly, is the basis of the kibbutz government, it is merely one item, albeit the most important, in the complex democratic administrative machinery which has been developed. The general meeting is best regarded as being the central feature of kibbutz democracy; below it are the various committees which actually run the daily affairs of the village in conjunction with the heads of the various branches of work; above it is the headquarters organization of the kibbutz federation with its numerous ramifications touching the affairs of each member-kibbutz at every point, and affording an immense reservoir of expert help and guidance. Headquarters is kept going by individual kibbutz members on loan to (or occasionally permanently taken over by) the head office.

In the early days of a kibbutz, little beyond the general meeting of all the members is required for its effective functioning. There will, of course, be a tendency for the workers in each particular branch to get together quite frequently. Some elementary committees will doubtless be found useful even at the start for regulating food, clothing,

and health matters. However, the organization will grow
rapidly, and matters will quickly become too manifold
and complex to be dealt with by the general meeting.

The secretary elected for the purpose of making official
contacts with the outside world, such as officials of the Jewish Agency's Settlement Department and of Government
departments, will quickly have to form a small secretariat
to help him. This will consist of the elected treasurer, the
farm manager (whose functions are essentially of a su-
pervisory and coordinating character), and one or two
other members charged with making purchases on behalf
of the kibbutz, and so on. In fact, almost the whole of the
subsequent organization in its essentials will arrive on the
scene very quickly, through the force of sheer necessity;
but it will all be on a small scale and will probably work
very informally. Some members will perform more than
one function, either because of an initial shortage of manpower, or because only a few members will have any clear
ideas about how to get the business going at the outset.
Then, as the kibbutz grows and develops, details requiring attention will multiply, large sums of money will
have to be attended to, and a full complex of committees
will have to be set up, complete with chairmen and perhaps even card indexes. Through their chairmen, who are
normally their spokesmen at the general meetings, all these
committees are responsible to the kibbutz as a whole, and
only small everyday decisions, without any serious general policy implications, will be made without the sanction
of the kibbutz in general meeting.

The "cabinet" of the kibbutz is the secretarial committee, which, in addition to the chief kibbutz officials,
numbers among its half-dozen or so members two or three
holding office "without portfolio" as it were, as general rep-

resentatives of the membership. Care is normally taken that women members be well represented on this central committee, and women kibbutz secretaries are quite common. This "cabinet" will present its proposals to the kibbutz through the secretary, who is generally, but not invariably, the chairman of the general meeting, and who gathers most of the proposals from the other, more specialized, committees. At its general meetings the kibbutz energetically discusses the motions put forward by the secretariat, and votes upon their adoption or rejection. A simple majority vote is normally sufficient, although, if attendance is relatively small and a serious matter under discussion receives a very small majority, it may well be agreed to defer final decision until later. The general meeting usually accepts the secretariat's proposals, although there are numerous exceptions to this generalization. Often the meeting, in effect, tells the secretariat to think again or even to drop its motion altogether. There can be no doubt about the reality of kibbutz democracy. If the general meeting is thought of as the kibbutz "Parliament," in contradistinction to the secretarial "Cabinet," it is a parliament without parties and pressure groups. In spite of a few inevitable human imperfections, and however deep and even bitter the differences of opinion that may from time to time be expressed very forcibly in it, the general meeting of the kibbutz is presumably the most perfect kind of parliament obtainable in the modern world, for, owing to overriding kibbutz loyalty, its solidarity is unshakable.

In the foregoing, the term "secretariat" has been used as synonymous with "secretarial committee," because this is how the terms are used in Hebrew. However, especially in a big kibbutz with a great deal of office business to transact, the actual secretariat, or office staff, is often bigger than, and largely different from, the secretarial committee. The actual office workers are distinguished from the wider functionaries by being termed in Hebrew the "technical" secretariat. As if to compound the confusion, the building in which the secretarial activities are carried on, whether a neat modern concrete office or a mere hut, is also called simply "the secretariat" in Hebrew.

In passing, one might perhaps mention the extreme importance of statistical work in the kibbutz secretariat. Quite apart from the annual balance sheet, drawn up under the auspices of an auditing organization which serves most agricultural villages in Israel, frequent data are compiled of the working time and investments in the different branches, of the production totals of the branches, their relative degrees of profitability, and so on. Since kibbutz members receive no wages but are remunerated in terms of goods and services, no money circulates within the kibbutz. For economic purposes, the kibbutz is one great household, and kibbutz accountancy is, therefore, a highly specialized subject. The value of a kibbutz "working day" must be assessed in terms of outside costs in order that comparisons may be made and effort and investment increased in one branch or reduced in another. The details can be passed over, but it must be made clear that kibbutz economics lie at the root of the work of most of the committees.

The secretariat, then, is the central coordinating committee. The other committees are those for health, culture, work, farm affairs, security, education, personal affairs of the members (including their housing and furnishing), absorption of new members, political activities, and village planning. Additional committees are set up if and when the kibbutz feels they are needed, including fairly in-

formal subcommittees, such as a temporary one for the arrangement of festivities. None of these committees should
be regarded as unimportant, as merely an expression of the
way in which the kibbutz apes the larger governmental institutions of the outside world. All of them are of vital importance for both the kibbutz as a group and the individual
members who serve on them. All the members of the kibbutz are individually affected by the committees' decisions
and turn to the appropriate committee whenever they are
in difficulties or have new suggestions to make. As far as
possible, over a period of years, almost every member is expected to serve on some committee. Some kibbutzim keep
a ten-year card index, showing the committee record of
each member. The social value of such participation in the
active government of a community cannot possibly be
exaggerated. It obviously instills a direct sense of public
responsibility in however modest a way, which elsewhere
only local councilors, an insignificant minority of the population, are likely to gain. Quite apart from the direct democracy of the general meeting, the kibbutz committees
thus afford an opportunity to virtually every member
(there may be a handful excused from committee service
for health or other reasons) to participate in local government. There is no finer way of learning the problems of
society today! The responsibility of the committees to the
general membership through the secretariat (which consequently involves the responsibility of the committee
member to himself as a kibbutz member—true self-government in the most direct sense!) ensures that every matter
is treated with the utmost seriousness. Although a committee decision or recommendation may be challenged
and rejected, it will not be because it is not worthy of serious consideration. Kibbutz committees commonly num-

ber about half a dozen members, but this, naturally, depends on the size of the kibbutz; a large kibbutz with several hundred members will tend to increase the size of its committees, including the secretarial committee, but a practical limit of around a dozen is soon set.

The question of how the membership of the committees is chosen is an interesting one. For this purpose, in fact, a special committee is elected, at the initiative of the secretariat, to receive nominations from the members and to make its own suggestions when necessary. This nomination committee has one of the hardest tasks of all in the kibbutz, for members by no means rush to offer their services—quite the reverse. There may be an occasional exception, but in general there is no lusting after power in the kibbutz, for the simple reason that a person who is ambitious or wishes to dominate others is not likely to become a kibbutz member. "Kibbutzism" obviously demands service and not self-aggrandizement. A self-centered individual, even if he did become a member in a kibbutz, is most unlikely to gain acceptance, since his personality would reveal itself during the trial period which is compulsory for all newcomers. A few exceptional psychological types of a rather domineering character may be found here and there in the kibbutzim; possibly they were accepted as members because of special services they had rendered the movement in the past or other unusual compensating reasons; but these are much too rare to change the general picture, which is one of a body of people highly unwilling to take office in individual capacities. This unwillingness can be regarded as both good and bad. It is good, insofar as it accords with the Platonic dictum that the best governors are the unwilling and, consequently, disinterested ones. It is bad, in that it causes difficulties in arranging for the smooth operation of essential services for the kibbutz. Owing to the nature of kibbutz society, storekeepers and committee chairmen are in close daily contact with all other members, often as a result of unavoidable conflicts of interest. Officeholders, therefore, are often, if not usually, in highly unenviable positions, and, unless they have real skill in handling people, they are likely to acquire a bad reputation. While this may be altogether unjustifiable, the fact remains that committee members, instead of receiving helpful encouragement often get just the opposite, tending to spoil the even flow of their own lives and damage their relationships with their fellow members. Also, it should be remembered that committee work is done in addition to regular daily work. To accept office in some sector or other of kibbutz life may be rewarding for its own sake, as a service to one's fellow men directly and as effectively as possible; but very often it is not looked upon in this spirit for the reasons mentioned. Perhaps more compensation should be given by way of reduced daily work; but, above all, laudatory recognition of the services of officeholders seems to be called for to a greater extent than is usual. It is noteworthy that in this matter the situation in the kibbutz is diametrically opposed to that prevailing in Western political democracy, where officeholding is commonly regarded as an addition to personal power and prestige. This clearly shows the difference between a society where "they" govern the people, in spite of being democratically elected, and one in which a small-scale, intimate, pure democracy obtains.

While it is not necessary to enter into the details of the work of all the committees, a few are of special interest. The work committee, for instance, stands behind that very important kibbutz official, the work-organizer. His work, usually carried out with an assistant, is generally regarded as the most onerous individual job of all. He arranges the work schedule of the other members, assigns everyone to a specified task, as far as possible with due regard to personal wishes, but mainly according to the demand for workers here or there. The more expert members naturally stay in their own branches of work most of the time, but others are switched about from day to day according to need. Complete records are kept of each member's hours of work (usually eight hours daily in winter and nine in summer). Those members who do not receive their weekly day off on the Sabbath get it on a weekday, or perhaps allow it to accumulate, and then travel for a few days. The general planning of the work, the special requests of certain members to work in certain places, queries and questions of transfer from branch to branch, are too much for the work-organizer to handle alone. He will, consequently, be guided by the work committee in regard to all these and similar problems.

In a comparable manner, the farm-affairs committee stands behind the farm manager and discusses questions of the expansion and contraction of the branches, investment in additional livestock and buildings, problems connected with transporting supplies and produce, the erection of fences, water supply, and innumerable other practical matters. After the secretariat itself, this is the most important of all the committees, since it essentially runs the business of the farm. If the kibbutz includes one or two industrial branches among its activities, their affairs too come within the purview of this committee. The general farm manager and his committee must also exercise some supervision over the various branches of services to members and children. In some kibbutzim such industries as soapmaking, the manufacture of electrical switches or water meters, fruit drying, canning or juice production, and so on, are of great importance as sources of income, and help provide light work for the older and weaker members. All this comes under the same committee system and, in complete defiance of general outside thought, succeeds with remarkable efficiency.

The committees and most of the officials are elected once a year, but, as stated at the outset, expert officials like the treasurer and farm manager will retain office for two or three years in view of the time necessary to train them before they can work effectively. This limited period of office prevents the development of a bureaucracy; there can be no established ruling class in the kibbutz, even apart from the fact that, every member being economically equal, no economic class differentiation can develop. Moreover, during his years of office, the kibbutz secretary must serve his occasional turns as waiter in the dining room or dishwasher in the kitchen just like any other member. In fact, even a kibbutz member who is also a member of the Knesset, the Israeli Parliament (and there are a few such members), is not exempt from such duties when he comes home from his parliamentary work in the capital. The kibbutzim insist that their democracy be all-embracing. Yet, in spite of this, questions do arise. There is a tendency for a rather narrow leadership group to rotate the main posts among themselves most of the time, with the kibbutz faithfully electing them to different posts every year or two. These members, among whom are found the foremost of the founding members of the kibbutz, undoubtedly form a kind of elite. They have no special privileges, apart from prestige and additional respect, not accorded to the ordinary member. It may be questioned whether this phenomenon does, in fact, detract from the reality of kibbutz democracy. In practice, a democratic society devoid of a leadership group is not likely to be firmly based or strongly progressive. This is borne out by the experience of those young kibbutzim which have not yet had the time or the good fortune to develop a qualified leadership. Equality is but a futile fetish if it is taken to mean that no man may outshine another, for there are, of course, immense differences in individual abilities. The essential requirement for pure democracy is that there should be no *closed* managerial class; the way should be *open* for every qualified person to rise straight to the top as soon as he convinces his fellows of his worth. Allowing for a degree of social inertia which makes it difficult for the newcomer to get accepted for the highest posts, simply because it is easier to vote for proven oldtimers, the kibbutz fulfills this requirement to the greatest extent possible in any human society. It provides a real basis of equality, the like of which cannot be achieved by society outside the kibbutz because of its competitive, individualistic nature. A leadership group not only does, but, for the sake of efficiency, *should,* exist in a kibbutz. It probably tends to be more fixed than may be considered ideal; but even so, it is always open to other members to supply fresh talent, and, in course of time, they are bound to do so.

The one serious weakness in the practical application of kibbutz organization is the sporadic attendance of most members at general meetings. There is a tendency for the general meeting to fall, all too fixedly, into the hands of a certain body of stalwarts who almost always attend, whether or not they center around the leadership group of the kubbutz (which is, of course, almost always present more or less *en bloc*). It is clear that these phenomena detract not a little from the reality of kibbutz democracy, and although they may be natural enough, they are none the less deplorable. It may well be contended that a member who does not attend the general meeting fairly regularly has no real conception of the kibbutz as a framework for life. An average attendance of three-quarters of the total membership at least would certainly seem to be desirable, instead of the mere one-third or one-half which usually forms the actual quorum. Care must be taken that the kibbutz avoids that unpleasant division into "we" and "they"—the governed and the governors—which detracts from the truly democratic character of most of the national political democracies of the world today. One cannot, of course, expect that a large majority of the members take a direct interest in the technical matters involving the various branches of kibbutz work which—after careful treatment in the relevant kibbutz committees— are bound to be brought before the general meeting for final decision. But the general meeting should, and nearly always does, receive a clear, general explanation of the issues from the secretary or from those specifically responsible in the matter. Greater efforts should therefore be made to assure a fuller attendance at the general meetings, in order to bring home to most of the members the responsibility of every individual for the decisions made, in which often very large amounts of money are involved.

It is not suggested that this weakness is so grave that kibbutz democracy is imperiled by it; there are many occasions when the agenda posted in advance on the bulletin board in the dining hall is sufficiently interesting to attract an adequate attendance. Moreover, one must not overlook the praiseworthy efforts of individual members to participate, not only in the voting, but in the discussions, in connection with matters far removed from their own spheres of work. A woman specializing in child care may, for instance, make highly relevant remarks about the suitability of a proposed new tractor for certain field work, either because she has picked up information about the matter from her husband or from someone else, or because a common-sense point occurs to her which the others may have overlooked. Such efforts contribute to making the kibbutz "parliament" the world's finest in miniature. It is not given to everyone to be an expert executive. But, as Pericles suggested long ago, it is open to every sensible democrat to make a personal reality of democracy by contributing to the general administrative formulation and direction of policy which affects each and every one, directly or indirectly. This is precisely what the kibbutz general meeting is for. Smaller, personal considerations should only exceptionally be allowed to interfere with its full operation. Improvement should certainly be sought for in this matter.

There is a tendency nowadays in the kibbutzim to raise the question of the power of committees as against the power of the general meeting. It is undoubtedly true that the development that has occurred in kibbutz democracy in this respect resembles that which has taken place in the larger field of political democracy outside. Government by decree, however, has not endangered either type of democracy, nor will it do so; what is happening is merely that a wide and apparently ever wider range of decisions on everyday affairs is reached in committee and put into practice without ever coming before the main parliament at all. That this is as inevitable in a large, old-established kibbutz, as in a national political democracy, cannot be denied. It would be quite impractical to overburden the general meeting with a mass of petty detail: moreover, the committees themselves are fully democratic in their organization. A degree of danger may exist: "Petty detail" may, here and there, be unduly expanded: but nothing indicates so far that reasonable limits have been exceeded, nor is the democratic common sense of the kibbutz likely to allow them to be.

Strong as the democratic organization of each kibbutz is, observers have rightly pointed out that the strength of the kibbutz movement as a whole lies in its strong tendency to federate. The three main federations, comprising some five or six dozen kibbutzim each (exact figures are not particularly significant, since growth is continuous), are *Hakibbutz Haartzi* (The National Kibbutz), *Hakibbutz Hameuhad* (The United Kibbutz), and *Ihud Hakvutzot veHakibbutzin* (The Union of Kvutzot and Kibbutzim). The first of these is associated with the Mapam, the second with the Ahdut Haavodah, and the third with the Mapai political party. To complete the picture, one must add the small orthodox religious federation, *Hakibbutz Hadati* (the Religious Kibbutz), along with two kibbutzim of Agudat Israel, and the few remaining kibbutzim which are independent. A complete list of the kibbutzim is given in Appendix II at the end of the book.

Hakibbutz Haartzi and Hakibbutz Hameuhad jointly maintain a very fine teachers' training college with two campuses, one outside Haifa and the other in Tel Aviv, for supplying personnel to their schools; the Ihud, whose political orientation is more towards the Center, has its own separate teachers' training college. Incidentally, all three major federations also participate in a fine amateur symphony orchestra, which rehearses and performs several times annually in different kibbutzim in order that the audience may come from a whole regional area. In spite of such examples of cooperation, each federation functions separately and independently, and, at the present time, it is impossible to foretell whether they will ever unite into one nationwide federation of all kibbutzim.

The kibbutz movement as a whole, nevertheless, stands solidly together, and is ready for joint action if, for instance, it feels its economic foundations threatened by unfavorable governmental policy as well as for a variety of noncontroversial activities. A very interesting point is that the three main federations regularly exchange their weekly printed and well-illustrated twelve-page bulletins, which contain news and articles about, by, and for the members of their kibbutzim. Each federation sends these bulletins to the main kibbutzim of the two other federations, where they are made available in the reading rooms. This procedure proves beyond a doubt that there is not the slightest tendency to conduct business in secrecy from rivals, as in the commercial world. Successes and difficulties are freely reported to all: kibbutz democracy is frank and open.

Incidentally, it should be mentioned here that inside each kibbutz great importance attaches to the mimeographed weekly or fortnightly bulletin (several kibbutzim have already reached the stage of printing it for their large membership), which provides news from all branches of the farm for those not directly connected with them, and which provides an open platform for members to express their views on kibbutz affairs in writing to all their fellows. A special committee acts as an editorial board for the production of this bulletin, which plays a very important role in democratic kibbutz life. Occasionally, the decisions of the weekly general meeting are also published in the bulletin, a practice which, this observer feels, is an obvious encouragement to the less active element in the membership to stay away from the meetings themselves. Information can, of course, be obtained by word of mouth in any event, but it is hardly likely that this would have the same undesirable effect as regular official publication.

It is usual for a large federation to have a main senior kibbutz which is its publishing headquarters, housing the printing press for the federation bulletin and other publications. But it is the Tel Aviv head office which actually manages the federation affairs, which affect all the member kibbutzim. Head-office activities are manifold, including advisory services for kibbutz agriculture and industry, education and household services, architecture, engineering (mainly in connection with water supply), building, all kinds of cultural activities (including, very prominently, study groups for ideological training of members), and a wide variety of guidance and assistance facilities to which every member kibbutz can turn at need. The personnel consists of a small permanent staff, including the leaders of the movement as elected and re-elected from time to time, some of whom, nationally respected, retain their positions unchallenged because they are known to be the best senior counselors available. In addition, expert and less expert officials are drawn on a temporary basis from among the kibbutz memberships themselves. Every kibbutz is obliged to send one member out of every thirteen or so to serve in some branch of the head office in associated federation work, which may include party political, newspaper, or youth-movement educational work. The terms of such service range from a few months to a

year or even more. The assignment often causes trouble
and difficulty for the member and his kibbutz, but it is a
burden which must be shouldered for the good of all. It is
possible to appeal against the demands made by the head
office, and the appeals are, at least occasionally, successful.
They are not made unnecessarily: every kibbutz knows
that it is a member of a large and strong group. The individual and his kibbutz are intensely integrated in the economic, political, and artistic life of the country through
the Histadrut, the great trade-union federation of which
every kibbutz member is automatically a member; they
share in its national health services, the Kupat Holim
(Sick Fund), they are served by the huge supply and marketing cooperatives; they are represented through the political parties; and enjoy the offerings of a range of cultural
institutions. Every kibbutz member knows that his life is
dedicated to the service of his fellows for the sake of common enrichment. All this results in an attitude of willing-
ness to serve the federated organization of the kibbutzim
even at considerable personal sacrifice.

Without going into the highly technical economic
details, it may be pointed out that the financial operations
and services of a kibbutz-federation head office are conducted on a large scale. The accumulated reserve funds
enable the federation to give loans and other low-interest
financial help to young kibbutzim struggling to establish
themselves. There is a standardized system of kibbutz accountancy. Based on the experience of many years of statistics obtained annually from the member kibbutzim, invaluable guiding norms have been established as to the
amount of money spent on feeding, clothing, housing,
insuring, etc., each adult member and each child; the

number of workdays each year to be devoted to household services and education, to the agricultural branches, and so on. There seems to be a federation norm for almost everything, including the maximum size of members' rooms and the standard amount of furniture to be found in them. The standard of housing and furnishing is one of the few things dependent upon a member's seniority in the kibbutz, nearly everything else being equal for all members, new or old. At the same time, there is no dictatorship involved. Any and every kibbutz can decide in general meeting to introduce for itself standards different from the ones accepted by the federation. Unfortunately, few kibbutzim are as yet so wealthy that they can afford to spend more on any one area than allocated by the norms; or, if a certain norm is exceeded in one field, it is only too likely that another norm will not be attained in another. In a word, the norms are sensible and valuable guidelines for each kibbutz. If norms are being exceeded, it will be a foolish kibbutz indeed which does not look into the matter seriously through its secretarial staff and the heads of the branches concerned. A small excess over the norm may not matter, as long as the kibbutz has a little in reserve; in fact, the richer kibbutzim may well afford to exceed norms within reason according to the general preferences of their members. In this way, norms of expenditure tend to rise, quite apart from the periodic adjustment necessary to take account of changes in national prices. Work norms, on the other hand, tend to fall as a result of improved and more efficient labor-saving methods. The head office, through its various technical branches, constantly arranges training courses to which the kibbutzim are urged to send members in order to acquire new and better methods. An improvement for one is an improvement for all: cooperation and mutual help are the watchwords. Kibbutz organization, both locally and federally, thus constitutes an effective example of democracy in action.

3

The Kibbutz and the Individual

The simplest way of setting the background for a consideration of the impact of the kibbutz on the individual is to describe a typical day in the life of a kibbutz member. It has certain resemblances to the life of any village agriculturist anywhere, but the differences are of far more fundamental importance.

Depending upon the season, the kibbutz member gets up between 5:00 and 6:30 in the morning, unless he has special duties at other hours such as milking or acting as night watchman or, of course, unless he has the day off. The usual thing is to go first to the dining hall to eat some bread and cream cheese or porridge and drink some tea. This does not take more than a few minutes, and then the member is off to work in whatever branch he is scheduled in. Either he is permanent in some definite work branch, or he is switched about according to need; in either case his name and work will be scheduled on the work bulletin board which is arranged the afternoon before, with last-minute amendments made in the evening after supper. Breakfast is normally at eight o'clock, but it is possible to eat earlier if necessary; very commonly, members do not find it convenient to leave their work before 9:00, hence the dining room is not through with breakfast much before 10:00. Kibbutz breakfast is not a very exciting meal; it almost invariably consists of raw vegetables in season, mainly tomatoes, also the not very hot Israeli peppers, and onions, bread, porridge, coffee or tea and the ubiquitous *lebeniah* (a kind of yogurt or sour milk), along with the usual cream cheese. After breakfast, work continues until noon, which is the standard kibbutz midday dinner hour, although dinner too extends until about 1:30. The midday dinner is the main meal and may comprise a modest portion of meat or a larger one of fish prepared in a wide variety of ways, together with cooked vegetables, usually potatoes, plus vegetable salad, soup, and, in the summer, possibly weak lemonade. There is always an alternative to the main dish for people who do not eat it, such as vegetarians: poached eggs or a cheese soufflé. Hard cheese—yellow cheese, as it is called in Hebrew, in contrast to the creamy white soft kind—is not common in the kibbutzim, as it is imported, but it does turn up at various meals on occasion. Work continues until about 3:30 or 4:00 P.M. in the winter; in the summer the usual quitting time is 4:30 or 5:00, or several hours later if there is a long midday break because of the heat. In the Jordan Valley, where midday temperatures in the summer are close to 100° F. for several months, a midday break of three hours is standard; it is obviously much better to work early in the morning and late in the evening. But it cannot normally extend very late into the evening, or there would not be time for the parents to be with their children for the customary couple of hours before bedtime. There is an informal afternoon teatime, called "the meal of 4:00" in Hebrew, when, upon concluding their daily work, members stop by the dining hall to have tea or coffee, with bread and jam. This is not a sit-down meal at laid tables, like breakfast, dinner, and supper, and some members, in fact, take the bread and jam to their rooms and eat there. Occasional snacks of this kind are often served also at informal evening gatherings in the rooms of personal friends, for which purpose cookies are periodically distributed. Otherwise all kibbutz meals are communal. The members have no fixed places in the dining room; as they enter they take the nearest available seat. Thus they have different eating companions every time, which is very important in bringing about mixing of the membership. One can, though, reserve a place for a husband or wife or some friend who is expected to join one, but, as a matter of fact, husbands and wives are often to be found seated by chance, at opposite ends of the dining hall, having come in from work at different times. In the evening, however, when they come from their homes they naturally sit and eat together. The typical table to be found in kibbutz dining halls is oblong, seating six, eight, or more; but some kibbutzim now adopt a more intimate arrangement of smaller square tables, seating four. Not all kibbutzim have as yet replaced benches by separate chairs, but there is steady progress in this direction too. Moreover, since many kibbutz dining halls are small, quite inadequate buildings with undersized kitchens, the strain on the kitchen staff serving food to the members is very great. Curiously enough, no cafeteria-type self-service system has as yet been attempted, although it would seem to be much more economical as far as manpower expenditure is concerned. Many kibbutzim do, however, insist that the members clear their tables and carry their used plates, etc., to a central collection point at the conclusion of their meals. Gradually dining rooms are rebuilt on a larger and pleasanter scale and in a variety of styles. Lack of funds, unfortunately, retards this development.

But the day of the kibbutz member by no means consists only of working and eating. After-work activities are extremely important, and depend as much on the personality and needs of the individual as they do in the outside world. However, in the kibbutz these activities usually take place within the framework of a large group of friends, subdivided into more or less intimate subgroups according to tastes. Nevertheless, one rarely encounters the development of definite cliques, because of the overriding active loyalty to the kibbutz as a whole. There is a tendency for a good many members to become so caught up in kibbutz affairs that they do not, in fact, enjoy enough uninterrupted time for the development of their own personality in certain individual ways, such as quiet reading or study. It is up to the member to strike a fair balance, but this is, no doubt, among the special problems of kibbutz life which are not always solved completely satisfactorily.

After the necessary visit to the showerhouse and change of clothes, there is not a great deal of time left in the early evening for personal activities. One has to tidy one's room and, if there is a garden around the block of rooms, one has to put in one's share in attending to it since the member who is the kibbutz gardener cannot do everything himself, not even with the help of the one or two members of the local youth group who may be assigned to work with him.

For anyone with children, the time between work and supper is sacred. They come from the children's houses to sit, play, and read with their parents in their room, on

the lawn outside, or on the general lawn of the kibbutz
near the dining hall. Soon it is time for the parents to
take them back to the children's houses to tuck them
in, say goodnight to them, and leave them in the care
of the night nurses on duty. Only a poet could describe
a typical summer evening scene in the kibbutz, with
the families resting in their deckchairs outside their rooms,
and their children playing happily at their sides, while
the sun slowly sinks behind the trees and the little
kibbutz houses. It is a scene of modern village beauty
without exact parallel anywhere.

Supper in the kibbutz is a smaller edition of the midday
dinner; it may well include an egg in some form, unless
eggs are provided at breakfast. The custom varies, but one
egg per member most days of the week is standard. The
poultry raising is one of the most important branches of
work, and a certain proportion of the eggs is retained for
home use, as is done with milk and vegetables. The usual
supper hour is 7:00 P.M. Youth groups generally eat at
6:30—not even in a large dining hall is there room for
everyone to be served together; or, if this is possible,
it is beyond the capacity of the kitchen staff to deal with
such a great number of people at once. Supper is served
up to about eight o'clock or so, or even later in summer,
to permit parents to spend the maximum time with their
children before supper.

As a rule, the dining hall remains a scene of animated
group conversation for some time after the meal, while the
work-organizer and the heads of the various branches arrange the work of the next day. The main consideration,
of course, is to obtain good results to be presented to
the appropriate committee in due course.

Apart from milkers, night nurses, night watchmen, and

workers on special night duties, the kitchen workers are the last to finish. They work in shifts, starting late if they are to continue later, or working a few hours in the morning and another few in the evening. Incidentally, they eat half an hour before the general membership, so as to be free to serve and wash up, during and after the official meal times. Finally, at about 9:00 P.M. the dining hall is clear.

It is around this time in the evening that the distinctive features of kibbutz life most typically manifest themselves. Up to this point, the day of the male individual in the kibbutz, apart from the communal eating and the general background of his particular form of village setting, has not been too different from that of rural workers elsewhere. As to the women, there is a more pronounced difference, because in the kibbutz they have no appreciable housework of their own, apart from tidying the room and playing with their children. They work during the day at the collective housework of the kibbutz, in the laundry, the kitchen, the children's houses, the sewing room and clothes store, or, not too often, in agricultural or industrial branches. In turn, a few men are always to be found in at least one or two of the household service branches—in the kitchen and the laundry where they are especially useful for lifting heavy items. However, the question of the woman in the kibbutz is so important that it will be dealt with separately later.

At any rate, after 9:00 P.M., both men and women reach the peak of the "kibbutzic" side of their life, for the late evening is the time for the many communal activities in which the full force of collective living is felt. There are committee meetings once a week; there are study groups; there are concerts, either played on the phonograph or, oc-

casionally, given by musically talented members; and
there are lectures by visiting authorities on subjects ranging from art to agriculture and archaeology. Such lecturers
are either invited independently by the cultural committee of the kibbutz, or, more frequently, sent by the
appropriate department of the head office of the federation, which also arranges concerts by touring musicians.
Payment is made by the kibbutz itself from the budget of
its cultural committee. There are showings, usually every
fortnight, of films made available by the Histadrut, not
only to the kibbutzim but also to the moshavim, so
that practically all rural Israel is covered. And there is, of
course, the general meeting of members, as a rule, every
Saturday evening. Occasionally, there will be visits to
a theater or concert in the nearest town, with groups of
members taking their turn some two or three times a year,
and transportation provided by the kibbutz farm truck or
by the local bus if available. In the case of special events
like these, supper will be served earlier to enable members to arrive at the place of entertainment by about
9:00 P.M., the usual curtain time for plays and concerts in
Israel. Now and again, a theater group will visit a
large kibbutz to give a regional performance, attracting
an audience from all the kibbutzim in the area. Or there
may be a visit to an amateur show of some kind in another
kibbutz, which may be so important as to draw a regional
audience of thousands. Any such event would necessarily
take place in an open-air amphitheater on a summer evening.

The various events are well spaced, and not many of
them occur in any one week. Nevertheless, the chances are
that, for many members, at least four evenings of the week
are filled in this manner. The result is that those deeply

involved in committee work or cultural affairs have difficulty in finding enough time for quiet reading or for some other individual and private activity. Moreover, there is the question of finding enough time for sleep—for even a kibbutz member must sleep! Meetings, as well as concerts and lectures, usually start at about 9:30 in the evening and go on until 11:00 or 11:30 P.M. Thus, not many hours are left for rest before work starts again early in the morning. Some members may have work schedules which enable them to sleep during part of the day, and a midday rest in summer is usual, but one pretends that this has the same value as a long, full night's sleep. The wise member will therefore, of necessity, curtail from time to time his evening kibbutz activities, so as to keep them within reasonable limits. It is truly a case of an embarrassment of riches. It used to be said in the earlier days of the kibbutzim that the young people seemed to work all day and dance all night. Folk dancing in the kibbutz, to the accompaniment of a piano, accordion or phonograph, is still of the greatest significance in maintaining the communal spirit in an atmosphere of great enjoyment; it takes place at the conclusion of every festive occasion, and provides a charming scene even for the bystander. Nowadays, however, moderation is more or less the rule; some members will attend some meetings, some others; some will have quiet evenings in their rooms or visit personal friends; others will retire to bed especially early. But on several evenings a week, the life of the individual in the kibbutz takes on a very different appearance from that of the private individual outside, whose evenings are as a rule spent quietly at home, apart from occasional visits to friends or performances. It is impossible to make a psychological assessment of the difference, but it is evident that the kibbutz member's entire life is different as a consequence of his spending his leisure time jointly with others in the community, in addition to the intensive contact with workmates during the day. There seems to be room for interesting psychological research to be done in this connection.

The general weekly rest day in the kibbutz is Saturday, regardless of whether the kibbutz is religious or not. A certain number of members must, however, work on that day, to feed and milk the animals, to maintain the village household services, and so on. They naturally receive some other day off instead. Sometimes members choose to save up their weekly rest days, in order to travel to town to visit friends or relatives, or to go on a tour; sometimes they may be requested to work continuously for a couple of weeks or so, if there are special difficulties in the branch, or if another worker is ill; the practice of working for long periods without rest days is, however, frowned upon. There are six holidays in the year, but more are to be added; in a rural life, though, a longer holiday is not as essential as in town. There is an arrangement for members over forty to receive one day's additional holiday for every year in excess of that age, so that later in life holidays are greatly extended. They may be spent quietly at home; used for touring or visiting; or spent in one of the beautiful rest homes that the kibbutz federations are now building for their members. In these rest homes a certain number of members can take turns every two or three years in spending a week in the modest luxury of their own "hotel" on the coast, on Mount Carmel, or some other beauty spot. Holidays need not be taken all together; they can be spread over the year, together with ordinary days off, but a whole week's break from work is considered advisable each year, perhaps more for the sake of psychological refreshment than from any pressing physical need. As the kibbutzim gradually become more and more prosperous, holiday time will undoubtedly increase. At present, during the long Israeli summer, working hours are still longer in the kibbutz than elsewhere, although in any such comparison it has to be taken into consideration that in the kibbutz, there is no journey to work and back and that time needed to walk to one's particular place of work, or to travel by tractor and trailer, is normally included in working time itself.

In every kibbutz a clinic is built, usually as soon as funds permit, under the auspices of the national Workers' Sick Fund, *Kupat Holim,* with one of the members functioning as nurse and in attendance at specified hours every day. In the clinic, members also receive dental treatment on specified days each week, and there is usually a sick room in which more serious ailments can be treated. Some cases can be and are treated in the member's own room. A special section of the kitchen provides suitable food for the sick, which the nurse or her assistants convey to them (chicken appears to be the standard kibbutz diet for sick persons). The health committee arranges for hospitalization and periods of convalescence in a rest home, if the kibbutz doctor (who may be a member and practice throughout the region, or who may visit on stated days from outside) confirms the necessity. There was one case where a kibbutz specially amended the building plans for a new dining hall in order to provide a low step that a crippled member could negotiate comfortably: in a word, there is no limit to what a kibbutz will do for the health of its members, and, of course, no personal cost is involved at all; it is a joint kibbutz matter.

Although the kibbutz member needs no money within the kibbutz, he does, obviously, require at least some cash for traveling outside. Through the committee dealing with members' affairs, he receives the equivalent of about thirty dollars a year. The exact amount depends upon the prosperity of his kibbutz, the younger settlements being able to give only the minimum. Little as this is, it is more or less enough for bus fares, one or two hard-covered books a year, or a greater number of paperbacks, and those few personal odds and ends which the kibbutz does not provide automatically because they depend essentially upon the taste or special requirements of the members (ranging from chocolate bars to ornaments for the room). The tendency is to increase the pocket-money allowance to the limit of financial ability, and although the kibbutz takes care of such matters as watch or fountain-pen repairs, it is obviously impossible for the kibbutz to meet every individual need. In the future, therefore, there is likely to be more and more opportunity for the members to foster their personal preferences more fully.

In the early days, any such move was apt to be frowned upon, as was the slightest tendency to so-called luxury; today, it is recognized that there is no reason whatever why the standard of living of the individual in the kibbutz should not rise continually, just as it does among those living outside who gradually increase their income. Time has shown that there is no danger that this development might affect the solidarity of the kibbutz spirit. Quite the contrary: a depressed standard of living is not conducive to that individual contentment which is the essential basis for a stable and happy kibbutz community. These days the committee for membership affairs concerns itself energetically with improving housing and furnishing, and securing radios for all members, or at least a system of loudspeakers in the rooms through which the member may select any program he wishes. There is no doubt at all that as soon as television arrives in Israel, the richer kibbutzim and, later, all of them, will buy sets; they will, in all probability, install a set with a large screen in a viewing room which will be open to all.

The question of accommodation for cultural and other activities is a pressing one in most kibbutzim: a good many have fine houses of culture, as the Hebrew title goes, but there is a great deal more to be done in this field. Meanwhile, all big meetings are held in the dining hall, which becomes the general village hall after 9:00 P.M., or else outside on the lawn, where film showings are held using a screen placed against a wall or strung between trees. Committee meetings may be held in the secretariat office, in a member's room, in a corner of the dining hall, or even in the library if the latter is not open at that particular hour. Of course, the library itself may be housed in an unused chickenhouse, or any other structure if the kibbutz has not yet succeeded in building a proper permanent home for it.

All this goes to show that, as far as physical conveniences are concerned, there are as yet considerable limitations and a certain scrappiness in kibbutz life, with the exception of the few really rich kibbutzim, which have taken thirty years or more to build up their prosperity in a hard land. But the social and cultural richness—in the kibbutzic sense one might almost say the spiritual richness—clearly more than compensates for all those who choose to live and work in a kibbutz. The general feeling is that members can wait several more years for the conveniences which they will really need only with advancing age. Of all the problems of the kibbutz, that of housing is the most pressing, for far too many members, even oldtimers, still live in huts or barracks which should long ago have gone the way of the tents of the early days.

In order to save money—the one commodity which is in short supply in even the richest kibbutzim—kibbutz travelers ride, whenever possible, free of charge in their own or someone else's farm truck, or utilize the services of any driver kind enough to oblige. Extended holiday tours of the country, even down to Elath, can be made this way. Almost every kibbutz in the country—as well as almost every one of the other more than five hundred villages— has good bus connections to the nearest of the three main cities: Haifa, Tel Aviv, and Jerusalem. With very few exceptions, chiefly in the remote Negev, buses are available every day, even if only once a day—from the kibbutz in the early morning and back in the late afternoon. An aerial observer flying over Israel at six o'clock in the morning would see buses crawling out of kibbutz farmyards and on to the road or track outside at a multitude of points all around the frontiers and including the most unlikely Galilean mountaintops, oases of cultivation in the southern sandy wastes, desolate locations in the Judean Hills, as well as from less romantic points closer to the center of the country, and gathering speed as they make their way to the cities. Those few kibbutzim which lie several miles from a highway bus route provide their own tractor or jeep connection down the length of their path, so that passengers can ride all the way to or from home. A good many kibbutzim are situated adjacent to main roads and enjoy bus service comparable to that of many city suburbs —perhaps half-hourly; others are served by three or four buses a day, and the remote ones, as already mentioned, by only one, perhaps even only once or twice a week.

Kibbutzim often include among their membership one or two bus drivers who, of course, pay into the coffers of the kibbutz all their earnings from the bus cooperative in which the kibbutz holds a share or two. They are typical "outside workers," as they are called, particularly valuable to the kibbutz, since they provide it with passenger transportation to the outside world. Lifts on trucks are, at best, somewhat unreliable (although at least one kibbutz now posts on its dining-hall bulletin board every evening details of the movements of its trucks on the following day, so that members know the possibilities for free travel). Moreover, work as a bus driver is very remunerative compared with the earnings of most kibbutz branches. Incidentally, it is quite possible also for other members of a kibbutz to work outside, apart from the quota at the federation head office. As a matter of fact, a certain number usually do work at a variety of outside posts, largely technical and often in some enterprise of the marketing cooperative which handles the kibbutz produce, or in some other undertaking in which the kibbutz holds shares. Such members are usually able to return home only on weekends, on account of the distances involved. The kibbutz treasurer or purchasing agent is often in a similar situation, spending much of his time in Tel Aviv, for instance, in negotiations on behalf of his kibbutz. Certain kibbutz members are musicians who travel all over the country to give recitals and return to their kibbutz home at irregular intervals. In general, however, outside work is not regarded with favor; it tends to lead to a position where the member only half belongs to the kibbutz, as it were.

In connection with the general question of travel, one might mention the possibility of going abroad, not merely for touring, although ideally that too should have a place, but for the purpose of visiting relatives in other countries. Only in exceptional cases of bad health or similar serious reasons can the kibbutz afford to give a member the allowance required; normally it will agree to do so only if otherwise it would lose the member, who might consider the trip so important that he would go to work outside to earn the money he needed. Even comparatively prosperous kibbutzim would have to be much richer before they could afford such expenditure for their members. In general, what happens is that the member's family overseas pays his expenses, and the kibbutz grants the necessary time off—a few months' leave is usual for America, for instance. When peace is finally secured with the Arabs, it is to be hoped that gradually all kibbutz members, along with the other inhabitants of Israel, will be able to enjoy inexpensive tours to neighboring countries.

So much, then, for a sketchy treatment of everyday life in the kibbutz. It remains to consider to some degree how far the average kibbutz member is affected by this specialized environment, with both its social and intellectual riches and its material restrictions. It would seem that the most important consideration in this connection is the individual's sense of values, for it is evident that the values of the kibbutz are quite distinct from those of the outside world. In the competitive world, ambition and aggressiveness are regarded as useful virtues; in the kibbutz, they would be quite unsuitable (at least in their raw state; it is conceivable that they could be sublimated appropriately). An individualistically ambitious person would not want to join a kibbutz, in any case. Both forms of society justifiably set a high value on personal warmth and pleasantness and on helpfulness; but the kibbutz, in contrast with the outside world, calls for an integrated outlook of cooperation, a sense of "we" and not only "I," although there is not the slightest demand that the "I" disappear. As the late Professor Joad of London University commented in his *Guide to Modern Wickedness,*

> From time immemorial men have belonged to social cliques and groups, each member of whom knew and was known by the rest. But in the modern large town, a man has a hundred different acquaintances, belongs to a hundred different units, with the result that most of his friends and acquaintances are unknown to one another. Now if one meets A, B and C today and foregathers with X, Y and Z tomorrow, and if A, B and C never meet and gather with X, Y and Z, then one misses the sense of belonging to a social whole whose being, just because it is more than the sum total of the beings of each of its members taken separately, informs and sustains the being of each of its members.

Dr. Joad was not referring to the kibbutz: he was analyzing the ills of modern urban society. But he could not have put more neatly the case for the kibbutz than in these striking sentences. In the kibbutz, a man is not less, but more, of a man because he is an active, responsible member of an in-group with which he interacts, contributing his own resources to it and deriving from it social sustenance. The properly integrated kibbutz member will have a quite different social outlook from that of the outside individual. He is not responsible, like the latter, only to his own family, but also to the coordinated group of friends of which he forms a part. His ties to his family are not weakened; on the contrary, they are strengthened by the feeling of total security which comes from his participation in the group; but he and his family have their being in a broader and deeper framework than that provided by the loose social organization outside.

Communal living in the kibbutz is calculated to bring out the best in men by emphasizing their interrelation, whereas competitive individualism is calculated to bring out their worst by making self-seeking their gospel. The significance of this point in regard to social morality cannot be overstressed. It is not to say that the social morality of the kibbutzim is impeccable—far from it. The kibbutzim exist in a capitalist world and must struggle to pay their way and provide an ever higher standard of living for their members. There is sometimes the same tendency to put the best vegetables on top of the box sent to market, in order to secure the highest grading (although the inspection at the receiving end is likely to go deeper than merely the top layer!), which occurs in the private methods of agricultural production. But, without going into the intricacies of moral theory, it may, perhaps, be commented that where the responsibility is shared, as in the kibbutz, communal faults are probably less serious than individual faults, although a communally shared crime is, naturally, as bad in itself as an individual one. The conscience of a community of a few hundred people working together can never be as black as that of a lone social desperado, for at least some in the group will be almost or quite upright and will accordingly influence the others either deliberately or unconsciously.

The kibbutz may not be perfect in its outside relations, because not all Israeli society is a federated kibbutz society; but it is bound to be almost perfectly fair within its own social structure, for any appreciable shortcoming would lead to friction and possible dissolution. As a matter of fact, criticism in the kibbutz is voiced so frequently and so openly that a casual visitor might think the membership was on the point of breaking up. The reverse is the truth, of course, and nothing could be more healthy than such open criticism. While outside the kibbutz such a procedure might lead to damaged social relations, within the kibbutz framework it actually cements the general social relationship by bringing disagreements out into the open.

The kibbutz community is one, and every member knows and feels it as such: this is both the strength of the kibbutz and the secret of its social control over the individual. In no place, perhaps, does public opinion count for so much as in the kibbutz. This expresses itself not only in the committees and general meetings, but also in daily conversation and, of course, in those subtle ways that work without words. It is not that members are unduly constrained. But a live consideration for the rights of others is imperative in an inclusive community like this, and it, in fact, becomes second nature in the end. The experience of the kibbutz shows that human nature, commonly supposed to be inveterately selfish, *can* be changed for the better, given a suitably moral social environment. One of the great problems of human society is how to balance the claims of the individual against those of society. Perhaps the greatest triumph of the kibbutz is its achievement of a happy balance in this respect: suitable social control of the individual without restricting his potentialities for self-development and -expression.

4

The Kibbutz and the Family

Outside the kibbutz, the immediate framework of individual life is normally that of the family. Although no
one challenges the position of the family as the basis of
our social organization, it is possible to question whether
the family is the ideal basis in itself. In the early days of
humanity some form of clan or tribe was basic; and to this
day there are many peoples whose way of life is based on
groups much larger than families: the extended family,
to be found in many parts of the non-Western world, is an
example. Particular interest attaches to the kibbutz in this
connection. In many ways it is not mere poetic imagery to
say that the kibbutz is like one big family; nevertheless, the
term is metaphorical: kibbutz families are as separate as
any others, but, at the same time, they do form one inclusive economic household as well as one inclusive fraternity,
and it is this economic and social unity which can solve
many of the troubles continually facing purely individualistic society.

It is because of this that such great sociological significance attaches to the kibbutz. Family intimacy and internal
interaction between parents and children, brothers and
sisters, normally tends to bring out the best in the related

members of the family in that give and take which is essential in coordinated living. In a similar way, conditions in the kibbutz are bound to strengthen and develop cooperative tendencies, so that the happy state in which personal freedom is dovetailed with social responsibility to produce a balanced and beneficial personality has every chance of being attained.

When considering the influence of the kibbutz on the family, and not only on the individual, it should be stressed that there are two reasons why the family alone cannot hope to reach such lofty social standards as the kibbutz achieves: first, it is as a rule too weak economically to attain that security which is essential for sufficient peace of mind to concentrate on social issues; second, it is much too small to serve as a breeding ground for social responsibility. Being set in a competitive society, the ordinary family is, to a large extent, a radically anti-social group, fighting its own battles and no one else's.

It is apparently not generally recognized that the chief characteristic of the private Western family working against the successful realization of its aims is its economic function, which interferes radically with what can be termed the pure family aspect—that of rearing children and providing a restful, recreational, and revivifying background for its members. In other words, the family is also a business. It must maintain itself economically, or face the frightening prospect of bankruptcy. This means, that— as in the case of the kibbutz or of any other economic group —economic considerations come first. For that matter, every human being must earn his living or be assured of his livelihood before he can start paying attention to higher human values, except for the few religious devotees and the handful of indifferent persons who leave everything to chance, on principle or without one. It also means that, unless the family is unusually lucky, it will not only be severely cramped by economic considerations, but will typically have little time, opportunity, or inclination left for more than a minimum of family affairs after attending to its economic considerations, which are all too likely to use up most of its energies. That is to say, the major efforts of most people must necessarily be directed to the prime task of keeping afloat, and their lives are but little enriched by the intellectual or other glories of our civilization at its best. In such circumstances, civilization is likely to be but a shallow thing, for it runs neither wide nor deep. The contrast with the living democracy of ancient Greece, even acknowledging the latter's restricted scope and limitations, would seem to be a painful if salutary one to draw. Among the achievements of the kibbutz is its management of economic affairs as merely one basic department of activity. It has succeeded in not allowing economics to overrun human life.

The effect of the kibbutz environment on family life is, if anything, still more profound. Whereas there are many individuals with special needs that even a rich kibbutz cannot satisfy, the kibbutz does provide the ideal setting for the family as such, enabling it to fulfill its functions in an atmosphere of cooperative security which cannot be bettered. The business side of life is attended to by the collective; the family is free to be purely a group where love and affection can reign, unsullied by the worldly cares which interfere with it in the outside world and, to a large extent, dictate the nature of its being. Insofar as business problems worry individual kibbutz members, they are shared by a wide circle of partner-friends, with the knowledge that, although there may be a period of hard times, neither the kibbutz federation nor, presumably, the Government would allow a kibbutz actually to go bankrupt. Relief loans, at least, are assured if a struggling young kibbutz finds that matters actually come to the worst in a new country with inadequate resources, and there is no question of kibbutz members facing destitution or anything remotely approaching it, as might happen in the case of a private farm family even in a modern welfare state. Thus the kibbutz can give the family what the latter cannot normally provide for itself—economic security—and, with it, thanks to the collective kibbutz organization, numerous opportunities for cultural activity, ranging from pottery to politics, as outlined above. Moreover, all this takes place within the framework of a community of numerous contrasting minds, working in cooperation, an environment too stimulating to permit the family to stagnate.

All this, however, is but the beginning of the matter. In fact, the kibbutz has not only provided an ideal setting for family life to flourish in, but has deeply influenced the form of that life in two ways. It has released the woman from the daily chores of housework, and, as a vital part of this process, has taken the children out of the home and placed them under the care of specially trained nurses and educators. As in the case of many of the other characteristics of the kibbutz, these apparently startling developments do not seem to have been devised deliberately at the outset; they arose from necessity, became standardized later, and were eventually incorporated into kibbutz outlook as an essential element of its way of life. When the first children arrived in the earliest kibbutzim two generations ago, it was found simply impracticable for every young mother to leave her work on the farm, the communal kitchen, the clothes store, etc. There was no alternative but to arrange for one of them to look after all the babies during the day, and for another to do so during the night so that the others could get uninterrupted sleep and be fresh for work on the following day. Thus began the kibbutz system of babies' and children's houses which has long since become a successful method of rearing children and of introducing them to democratic principles at an early age. It involves, in fact, a "children's society," as it is called, in every kibbutz. The importance of the rapid humanizing and socializing effects of this system is not yet fully appreciated by educators in general. It goes far beyond the modest advantages of the creche, or even of the boarding school, with which it has a superficial similarity. Thus the women and the children in the kibbutz are more deeply affected by its way of life than the adult males. For them family life is something radically different from what they would experience outside.

The whole question of the position of the woman in the kibbutz and of fully satisfying her psychological needs looms large and has not yet been solved satisfactorily. In fact, it is the subject for energetic current sociological research within Hakibbutz Haartzi. The main aspects of the problems involved will be outlined later and only the family aspects will be touched upon here.

The kibbutz mother is very much in the position of the working mother anywhere, with one important difference. Outside the kibbutz the mother is beset with worries about the care of her children while she herself is at work. Possibly even more bothersome is the problem of how to take care of the children after she comes home from her daily work and yet be fit to go back to work on the following day. In the kibbutz, she is relieved of all these worries. She enjoys the same security which the kibbutz gives to its members in all departments of life. To the obvious criticism that children should not be separated from their mothers as they are in the kibbutz, there are two convincing answers. Firstly, with the exception of a very few cases, almost invariably occurring among children entering the kibbutz at an advanced age, no bad effects have been observed, while, on the contrary, many good ones have come about. Secondly, the well-to-do mother in private life habitually hands over her children to the care of nurses from the earliest age and usually sees them only at prearranged periods when she and they are at leisure; this is precisely what happens in the kibbutz, whose children are, in fact, treated just like those of the wealthy.

This is true in the material sense too. Although as far as the adult members are concerned the kibbutz must limit the standard of goods and services, practically nothing is denied to the children, who are the pledge of the future on whom depends the fate of the movement. Consequently, the expenditure on the housing, clothing, feeding, and care of the children is far in excess of adult standards, with special head-office norms, and is not infrequently increased at the expense of all other budget items. For children the kibbutz is, in any case, a paradise; supervised by expert nurses, they spend their early years playing and learning in interesting and pleasant rural surroundings. It is not surprising that kibbutz children are known throughout the land as prime specimens of Israeli youth.

This is not to say that there are not a good many difficulties in connection with their upbringing, as in the case of children everywhere—difficulties both psychological and physical, requiring special attention. Cooperation between parents, nurses, teachers, and the doctor is easier and closer in the kibbutz than it can ever be outside in the very nature of the case. There is no difficulty in making special arrangements suggested by experts. Instead of the limited resources of the individual family, the much larger economic capacity of the whole kibbutz stands behind each child and parent. Mothers whose children need them for extra care are immediately granted the necessary time off from daily work. Although the kibbutz subscribes to the principle that it does more harm than good for parents to interfere too frequently with the nurses' work, the children's houses are, in practice, always open to parents.

Child care can be a very complex affair, and the kibbutz can afford to let those of its members with special aptitude attend advanced training courses arranged by the federation, and thus attain a standard of competence few outside mothers can hope to rival. Also, the kibbutz mother can devote more time to her children and give them her attention more fully than can the harassed mother in the individual family, who is rarely free from household duties and frequently uncertain of obtaining a proper night's rest. In view of all this it is not surprising that kibbutz children reach the highly satisfactory standards noted by innumerable observers. Moreover, the atmosphere surrounding them, in the social sense, can hardly be duplicated outside. In addition to the essential sense of belonging to their own families, they are also "our" children, the children of the kibbutz as a whole. Everyone takes an interest in them and is ready to show them a new farm animal or tractor, or give them a ride in a cart. Child rearing in the kibbutz is not perfect, no more than is anything else, but it is difficult to determine now what additional efforts could be made, and in what directions, in order to improve it.

The higher the private family's own cultural level, the more difficult the problem it has to face and solve in providing what it regards as the best educational opportunities for its children. The kibbutz was founded, developed, and maintained largely by people of high educational background in Europe, including a considerable percentage of university graduates. Consequently, the education of kibbutz children has received very close attention, and a unique system has been devised, calculated to produce a new kind of rural worker both deeply attached to his communal village and with a wide general culture.

There has been, it is true, a certain reaction against giving children university education. In general, the immigrants who came to Israel to find their freedom in a new way of life in the reborn ancient land, the ancestral home of their people and the focus of their modern national aspirations, reacted against the typical Diaspora social structure of the Jewish people characterized by a preponderance of the professions and middleman occupations. The philosophy of A. D. Gordon, emphasizing the value of physical labor, became generally accepted, and early kibbutz members tended to sneer at their own fine education and to regard it almost as a shortcoming. Clearly, this was going too far, and in most cases it has been replaced by a more reasonable view. But the fact remains that kibbutz education bears the stamp of the Gordonian philosophy of labor and minimizes the theoretical in favor of the practical. There is no objection whatever to a kibbutz member specializing in, say, some phase of world literature as a hobby; but there is no endeavor to train a kibbutz child deliberately in any such subject, which cannot be said to help him to be a more valuable kibbutz member when he grows up. On the other hand, a child's talent for painting or music is regarded as being of value in later kibbutz life, and such talent will therefore be fostered to the utmost with anything ranging from private lessons to eventual study tours abroad. Talents for such arts rank, in the view of the kibbutz, with a predilection for soil chemistry or mechanics, which are obviously worth fostering from the outset.

Another reason why very few kibbutz children ever reach the Hebrew University or the Technion is that, in order to gain admittance, one must pass the usual school examinations, and kibbutz schools neither believe in nor hold such examinations. The whole outlook of the kibbutz, which wishes to bring up its youth in an atmosphere of cooperation and not competition, militates against examinations. Untiring personal attention is devoted to the children's progress in their studies, and serious discussions are held and reports made about it; but the holding of examinations and the awarding of marks are not countenanced because of the competitive atmosphere they necessarily engender. Only in those very rare cases, where a child is so gifted that university education is clearly essential for him and his achievement may redound to the credit of the whole kibbutz will special arrangements be made for him to take the necessary outside examinations.

Kibbutz education has become a highly specialized and most fascinating branch of pedagogy. It merits detailed treatment, but only the barest outline can be given here. It is based on a grouping of the kibbutz children into age grades, usually of about six individuals who grow up together as they pass from kindergarten to succeeding classes. The ideal is for one nurse to care for them through the early years. Each children's house comprises a dining room, a classroom, and bedrooms. No separation of the sexes has been found necessary until the late teens in this completely coeducational system. Year by year the class moves up allowing, of course, for any special adjustment in the case of a particularly backward or precocious child, who may be transferred to another class. Thus the children progress until the age of eleven, when transfer to a regional high school takes place and kibbutz secondary education may be said to begin. The "project" method is used almost exclusively during the period of elementary education and even afterwards; that is to say, the class is given one or more projects a term, such as "Haifa Port," "The Post Office," "The Ancient Tribes of Israel" or "Water." Within the framework of any such project, all the main subjects of the curriculum can be taught without the children noticing it, as it were. In accordance with kibbutz principles, the children contribute compositions, songs, drawings, etc., to a communal class notebook; later, the sheets are bound in volumes and displayed in the term-end exhibition which parents and other kibbutz members visit with deep interest and pride. Arithmetic, geography, history, and, of course, reading and writing, in the later stages in English as well as in Hebrew, and other subjects such as nature study, are all incorporated in the projects. The children's interest is stimulated to a practical end all the time, and it is, of course, at the discretion of the teacher to dwell upon whatever aspects seem to be insuf--ficiently grasped by the children.

Ordinary teacher-pupil relationships are not found in the kibbutz classroom. The teacher is essentially the guiding leader of cooperative work, is called by his first name, and in general acts in accordance with the best principles of progressive experimental schools. In the kibbutz, however, the matter has gone far beyond the experimental stage and is now successful standard practice. The project method arises naturally from the constructive play-work of the kindergarten and is developed from this to lead the child naturally through the years of elementary education until he is ready for a more advanced stage. By that time he will have absorbed the principles of practical equalitarian and cooperative democracy, since not only is classwork collective, but democratic ideas are instilled from the outset. The children themselves consider breaches of rules in the children's house by sitting in committee, as it were to discuss them, and arrange any necessary punishment under the guidance of the teacher or nurse.

Secondary education in the kibbutz is considerably more extended than in the outside world, although it does involve part-time work in the kibbutzim themselves as well as in the children's farm attached to each regional high school. It covers the 11 to 18 age group. Work starts very gradually, at first, only an hour or two, and progressing to half days at the end. This method of introducing the child to the adult working world in easy stages eliminates the abrupt change facing the ordinary outside child, who, on leaving school, is plunged into full-time work and an altogether different associated life, with rarely any psychological or physical preparation whatever. The purpose of kibbutz education is to prepare the child for intelligent kibbutz life in the future, and the entire system has been geared to this end.

The regional high schools are boarding schools, where the kibbutz child enjoys the privileges preserved for children of rich families in the outside world. The child returns home to his own kibbutz every weekend, so as to be with his parents on Sabbaths, the regular day off from work. If the regional school happens to be in his own kibbutz, the child is not far from his parents in any case and may see them during the week as well; but even if the regional school is far away, regular transportation is provided. Schoolwork largely follows the familiar lines of the project method, and the same cooperative class notebooks are produced, but the subjects are studied as subjects. The study of English literature in English may not run very deep, but high standards are attained in chemistry, biology, and other agriculturally oriented sciences in particular, as well as in political theory, reflecting the political outlook of the federation. The term-end exhibitions, expanded in the higher grades to striking proportions, show an extent and range of achievement which must be seen to be believed. Special emphasis is given to handicrafts, and, here too, the standards attained—in woodwork, metalwork, leatherwork, embroidery, and other applied arts, to say nothing of the fine arts, drawing, painting, musical and dramatic performances—would do credit to teenagers in any part of the world.

In some ways, kibbutz education is deliberately limited in scope, but it is clear that it does give the child unfettered liberty for the development of his talents, which is surely the purpose of all education. Obviously, such results can be achieved only through the efforts of expertly trained teachers, and it is thanks to the kibbutz teachers' seminars, previously mentioned, that such high standards can be attained. Incidentally, sports, of such great importance for the health of the young, are given all the attention they deserve. When the warm Israeli climate prevents athletic and similar activities in daytime, floodlit sportsgrounds enable them to be carried on in the cool evenings. Basketball is the favorite kibbutz sport, and kibbutz teams, built up into strong leagues, also play against town teams. In so harmless a field as sports, competition is not ruled out even in the cooperative kibbutz, it being realized that there are indeed certain areas where competition brings out the fullest capacities of the individual.

All things considered, kibbutz education, with all its limitations as compared with the full array of university courses available for the most fortunate young people outside, is remarkably comprehensive. In addition to all the foregoing, it includes practical introductions to numerous types of kibbutz work, beginning with the little flower-and-vegetable plot the young children have next to their houses together with a few goats, rabbits and/or other semi-pet animals to care for, and ending with the scientifically run and expertly guided regional school farm and workshops and in the kibbutz itself. With all this, the average kibbutz teenager will easily hold his own in comparison with his outside counterpart in general knowledge of world literature and affairs, an acquaintance with the history of art and music, a fair idea of the salient points of social, political, and economic theory, and so on. In fact, considering the usually high cultural standard of the kibbutz, he will often be better informed about general culture than his middle-class counterpart outside. Kibbutz parents certainly have no cause for worry over their children's education. At the end of high school, and to some extent at earlier stages as well, considerable touring and traveling in the country are arranged, so that children can examine for themselves the life of the towns and of the private villages. In some instances they may even live outside the kibbutz for a year; and, in any case, they have to serve their period of compulsory military service, a part of which is devoted to agricultural work, carried out under military conditions in some other kibbutz.

Where the system of kibbutz education is intensive, as in the case of Hakibbutz Haartzi, the number of children leaving their kibbutz when they finish their education is close to nil, except for those who go to found a new kibbutz in a previously undeveloped region of the country. In the other federations, it is sometimes considerable, which only testifies to the freedom prevailing in the kibbutz world: every member and every member's child is free to leave any time. In practice, however, the entirely voluntary system is more than self-sustaining, and nowadays the kibbutz children constitute the main source of future growth in membership. There can be no better testimony to the success of kibbutz education than this happy phenomenon.

It is the natural wish of every family that its children should both follow its traditions and improve upon them. One of the functions of education is certainly to fulfill this wish, although it may not be generally realized how closely educational systems do, in practice, accord with the aims of the society in which they function. Western competitive society in general maintains educational systems which, through their competitive marks and examinations, inculcate into the children during their formative years those attitudes to life which are appropriate for the continuation of that society in its prevalent form. It is therefore not at all surprising—on the contrary, it is inevitable—that kibbutz society, cooperative to the core, should adopt an educational system contrasting in many ways with those prevailing in the Western world at large.

Kibbutz society too depends fundamentally on a method of education for its children suitable for its furtherance. The choice of an appropriate educational system was made deliberately, since the early members knew perfectly well that their social requirements were by no means identical with those of the surrounding world. Consequently, kibbutz education is carried out within a special cooperative framework, and is, in fact, known as "cooperative education." The name is wholly justified, for it is cooperative not only among the children themselves, who remain in their close groups throughout their school years and, following them, even go through their army period together. It is cooperative also in the sense that parents and teachers participate in it to an extent which cannot be duplicated outside. In some cases, some of the parents are themselves the teachers (a phenomenon very rarely met with elsewhere) and, in any case, both parents and teachers are members of the same kibbutz, in constant personal and committee contact as their daily lives dictate. That constant cause of grievance to teachers outside—clashes with the ideals, if any, of the parents, whose influence often pulls in a direction completely opposed to the highest aims of the teacher—cannot occur in the kibbutz. Differences of opinion are smoothed out in private or committee discussion, for both parents and teachers are members of the same kibbutz and can therefore have only a joint overriding kibbutzic aim.

Kibbutz education is different from other education for both practical and theoretical reasons. In the first place, the child's practical tendencies must be developed to the utmost in order to enable him to become a productive member of a working rural community. Secondly, he must be given the theoretical background of kibbutzism as a way of life, with all its social and political implications, its history, and its aims, so that he can grasp its special significance and dedicate his life to its furtherance. If, in the end, for temperamental or other reasons, which may apply to anybody, he rejects the way of life for which he has been educated, this in no way denotes that either he or the system is a failure; it merely signifies that in certain instances the budding human personality needs to find its way independently of its background. This, of course, happens just as much outside the kibbutz framework as within it; there is always a certain small proportion of individuals who break away entirely from the trend of their upbringing. But, as has been mentioned, such exceptions are very rare indeed where kibbutz education is very intensive—a matter which, no doubt, is paralleled outside.

The basic point is that kibbutzic education has an orientation all its own, even in dealing with themes which are common to all education in the country, and, to a large extent, outside it. For instance, the Bible is just as much an everyday book for study in kibbutz schools as in others, but in the nonreligious kibbutzim it becomes the background textbook for the history and geography of the country. The children, naturally, imbibe simultaneously its moral teaching as well. In the religious kibbutzim, on the other hand, with their ideology, the Bible is the basic item of instruction, and its contents are interpreted in their full religious significance within the framework of communal life, in a way which, again, has no exact counterpart outside.

In ordinary, non-kibbutz schools too, the best teachers try to inculcate into their pupils a sense of duty to their country and people; however, all such efforts must run

counter to the general tendency of individualist society because narrow-minded, selfish careerism often appears, to
the individual who wants to get on in the world, as the only
path to follow, and parents all too commonly foster this attitude. In the kibbutz, however, there is a natural harmony
of ideas of service; parents and teachers work together
within the same cooperative framework to implant in
the child a sense of service not only to his own kibbutz and
its federation, but, beyond the kibbutz movement as a
whole, to the entire people in whose recent history the kibbutzim have played such a vital part.

Formal education completed, and the period of army
conscription finished, the young person returns to active
participation in communal living and, in the course of
time, marries and carries on the family cycle of the generations.

Adult education is continually in full swing in the kibbutzim; various study circles are formed every winter, and
members are frequently sent to attend short or long study
courses and seminars for all kinds of training as needs and
inclinations dictate. As the couple grows older, they gradually retire from work, and continue to live comfortably
in the kibbutz, adequately maintained by the productive
work of their sons and daughters.

It has been observed that inter-kibbutz marriages are
more frequent than intra-kibbutz ones, a tendency which
probably continues. Kibbutz youth has many opportunities
for making outside friendships, not only in the army, but
in the various gatherings which are arranged for the upper
grades in the regional high schools, as well as in youth
camps and tours. A serious problem to be solved in inter-
kibbutz marriages is, of course, which kibbutz the couple
will choose to settle in. There is no hard-and-fast rule in

the matter; all kinds of considerations, including consideration for parents, play a part. Since there is as yet no civil marriage in Israel, even in a nonreligious kibbutz the couple must go to a rabbi to be married, following which the kibbutz arranges a festive gathering in their honor. In a religious kibbutz, the full traditional wedding ceremony is, of course, performed, possibly in a town synagogue if the parents happen to belong to one. The most serious difficulties in connection with marriage occur if one of the partners is not a kibbutz member. As far as possible, every effort will be made to incorporate the pair into the kibbutz, but there are instances where this cannot be done and the young man or woman is lost to the kibbutz. But where all goes well from the kibbutz point of view, the way is clear for a further increase of kibbutz population amid general rejoicing. Family planning is a matter for general kibbutz discussion, according to economic resources; the richer kibbutzim are now able to allow up to five children per family, so that the limitations imposed are certainly not stringent. As the years go by, the population of the children's houses is renewed, and there is another "Pine" group, another "Lily" group, another "Rock" group, in accordance with the charming kibbutz custom of giving the children's groups poetical names which remain with them throughout the years of their youth. Thus the kibbutz family's life continues on its rewarding way.

5

The Woman in the Kibbutz

In contrast to ancient Greece, where the woman was not enfranchised, in the kibbutz the ideal is complete equality for the woman in every aspect of full kibbutz democracy. Nothing less can satisfy the equalitarian demand for total respect for the human dignity of every member. Complete political equality does, of course, exist, except insofar as women members are sometimes inadequately represented on committees and in the higher official posts—a matter for constant future attention; and except insofar as they do not always take full advantage of their rights to speak and vote—a matter for their own constant attention.

Nor is there any question about their complete social equality in all ways. The chief difficulties lie in the sphere of work, and it cannot be pretended that the position is satisfactory in this regard. By the nature of the case, it is far from certain that complete satisfaction ever can be achieved; but it is acknowledged that there is room for improvement. The problems are far from simple, and fully justify the special attention being given to them now. To mention only one instance, in the head office of Hakibbutz Haartzi a special department has been set up to deal with matters affecting women members.

In the early days of the kibbutz, when the first youth groups imbued with the new ideals started striking roots in the Jewish homeland reborn essentially through the work of their hands, the women were immediately given full equality in work as in everything else. But this attempt to solve the age-old problem of woman's inequality was not an immediate success. Although a good many of the young women did, in fact, succeed from the outset in various agricultural pursuits, it has also been noted that there was much overtaxing of strength which, in some cases, led to injurious results. There are still a few women working as tractor drivers (not that tractor driving is necessarily among the heaviest jobs) , but they are rare enough to be the occasional subject of journalistic comment. In addition to their traditional rural occupation of milking, now increasingly mechanized, the female agricultural workers in the kibbutz are nowadays usually found in the chicken-house (also a traditional feminine occupation on a small scale in the past), the orchards, the tree nurseries, the vegetable gardens and, very prominently, in the light industries carried on in the kibbutzim. For security reasons, it has up to now not been possible to use women members as shepherds to any great extent, but there have been a few who achieved kibbutz fame and more; given better conditions in future, there is certainly scope for development in this regard.

Apart from these branches, the place of the woman in the kibbutz has usually been within the framework of child care and education, and household services in general. In other words, the kibbutz ideal of the complete emancipation of the woman from housekeeping duties beyond the essential minimum has not been attained. However, the question arises as to whether its achievement would be desirable either in principle or in practice. It is true that the number of women in the agricultural and industrial branches might well be increased, although the practical problems in the way of such increase are very great. As to household services, in the kibbutz they are very different from private housework; many of them, by virtue of being collectivized, become quasi-factory occupations. Acknowledgment of this fact, though, does not mean that all the problems are solved. To move from housework into quasi-factory work is, indeed, for many women, merely to jump from the frying pan into the fire. This in itself is one important aspect of the whole problem of how to find a really satisfying place for the woman in the kibbutz. For, in spite of the many, many thousands of happy feminine lives achieved in the kibbutz, a certain measure of dissatisfaction does exist, and it is for this very reason that more serious efforts than ever before are now being made to deal with the matter.

It is comparatively easy to tackle the problem in words: it is more difficult to apply theoretical solutions in practice. It has been said many times that the status of women's housework in the kibbutz scale must be raised; that there must be much more rationalization of labor, more participation in training courses, and better organization in general. Such occupations as laundry work, clothes sorting and repairing, cooking, and even cleaning can and should become professional occupations, of equal status with agricultural activities. There is a good deal of truth in this, but it is far from being the key to an over-all solution. Head-office kibbutz federation departments have long existed to guide the member kibbutzim in the direction of greater and greater improvements in work organization. Much mechanization has already taken place and it progresses steadily. Many kibbutzim for instance can boast the latest in laundry and kitchen machinery.

But the matter boils down largely to a question of social status. There is an unmistakable tendency in many cases to look down upon household services in the kibbutz as being unproductive, since they do not produce revenue. Consequently, the members—mostly women—who work in them tend to develop something of an inferiority complex. It is not that they actually do not enjoy a social status equal to anyone else's in the kibbutz; it is rather a matter of feeling. But because it is an intangible psychological manifestation, it is no less serious, and, in fact, much more difficult to deal with than some practical issue calling for adjustment.

Deliberate efforts should be made in kibbutz administrative circles—especially in the secretarial committee—to pay more attention to the household branches of kibbutz work; to give increased internal publicity to their achievements, largely lacking altogether at present, both in the kibbutz magazine and on the general bulletin board; and to arrange lectures and discussions not only for the workers in the household branches themselves but for all kibbutz members whose well-being depends on efficiency in the household services. In such ways, understanding could be increased, sympathy gained, and the atmosphere changed. The problem of atmosphere is of particular importance, since public opinion in the kibbutz often tends to overcrystallize—an unavoidable disadvantage of a small, closed society which is more than compensated for in other respects. This whole matter calls for an energetic and imaginative attack.

So much for the collective aspect of the psychology of the women's problem in the kibbutz. The individual aspect—that of the psychological satisfaction of the woman member herself—is at least as difficult, since it touches the roots of her personal life and outlook. However dangerous it is to indulge in generalization this is one of the cases where it is unavoidable. It is probably more difficult for most women to accustom themselves to kibbutz life, even when very young, than it is for most men. The feminine temperament, with rare exceptions, is more passive, more homebound, less adventurous, although this is offset by a greater readiness on the part of most women to serve a cause to which they are devoted. The fact remains that, in general, the kibbutzim suffer from a shortage of women which, of course, affects the kibbutz social structure and, in the most serious cases, even its stability.

There is a good deal of substance to the belief that it is more difficult for a woman than for a man to find complete satisfaction in the kibbutz, unless, of course, her personal relationships within the kibbutz are ideal for her. The belief is growing that the private housewife actually enjoys her almost constant work and worry entailed by her taking care of her house, husband, and children. Sometimes she frankly admits that this is the case. If this be so, the kibbutz has a difficult task indeed in trying to give its women substitute psychological satisfactions which would make them fully contented members. One thing is certain: there is no need to introduce artificial worries for the sake of feminine satisfaction. There is a sufficiency of worries of various kinds in every kibbutz, as in every social group. The answer may lie more in the direction of a conscious reorientation of outlook: the woman should shoulder more and more internal social responsibility. It may seem to be going rather far to suggest that in certain areas women should be the natural leaders of the kibbutz community;

and yet it may be that something like this would prove the most promising approach. The kibbutz is a revolutionary form of society in any case; and if it set out more deliberately to reverse the usual run of things outside, where men dominate in almost every sphere, it might come up with some really significant solutions and, at the same time, make a further striking contribution to pure democracy in practice. This is not the place to discuss the question whether the insufficient participation of women in politics and public affairs in general has facilitated wars and other social evils, but the kibbutz would appear to be the ideal place for consciously experimenting in the opposite direction to a greater extent than has yet been tried. There is no danger of overdoing it, since many, if not most, women are naturally of a rather retiring disposition; on the other hand, various social advantages might result. One cannot expect that women will come flocking to the kibbutz from the outside, even if it became generally known that the kibbutz was something of a feminine paradise; but some stimulus to female recruitment might result from the pursuit of such a policy.

The practical forms which a policy of this kind should take are matters for future discussion within the kibbutz movement. Current research, designed to reveal the roots of the problem, must first be completed, but some of the more obvious possibilities can be suggested now. These would include the greater participation of women in committees and administrative posts; the formation of special groups and the holding of special meetings from time to time for women members for discussion and subsequent action in matters such as increased social amenities in the kibbutz; and the arrangement of additional amenities for women workers, such as recorded "music while you work" in the sewing room and other places, which would stimulate and not interfere with work. (Music, incidentally, has been employed in the cowshed.)

Women are not going to be attracted to the kibbutz, and, if they come, are not going to find full satisfaction in it, if household work is merely collectivized into quasi-factory work and if other occupations are few and far between. Nor is there any particular attraction in their changing over from outside factory, shop, or office work to its kibbutz counterpart, unless they simultaneously appreciate and enjoy the advantages of kibbutz life, its companionship and security, to the same full degree which, for psychological reasons, comes more easily to men. Consequently, it may be worthwhile to work out an additional special educational program for women, in the preparatory youth movements, as well as afterwards in the kibbutz itself. It has already been suggested that the general trend of girls' education in the kibbutz regional high schools should be considerably altered, for at present they are brought up, for the most part, with the idea that the ideal of kibbutz work is agricultural or industrial productivity, only to find later on that in practice there are not enough places for them in the directly productive branches. This leads to a great deal of unnecessary disappointment and dissatisfaction, including possibly leaving the kibbutz. A different educational orientation, concentrating on the specially important part women can play in other work fields, would doubtless alter these unfortunate results for the better. Nor does there seem to be any reason why specialized training, for instance, in general nursing and child care should not begin in the last years of the kibbutz schoolgirl's education, instead of requiring her to give as much time as the boys to the school farm, although her future will probably not lie in agriculture at all.

Discussion, however brief, of the woman's place in the kibbutz cannot omit some mention of that important feminine subject, dress. Here again, in the early days, the approach to the subject was somewhat overrevolutionary. Work clothes must naturally be as simple as possible, but even after working hours the simplicity was overdone, and, until recently, complaints of drabness were still heard in some quarters. In most cases, though, the situation has long since changed, and the quality and individual variety in dress among the women today is indeed remarkable; much of it is a tribute to the talent of the members themselves. When she visits town, the kibbutz woman is indistinguishable from any other middle-class woman as far as dress is concerned. On festive occasions, brilliant effects are achieved by the bright embroidery of the Eastern European or Yemenite styles often to be seen among the women—and, more rarely, also among the men, whose decorated shirts are scarcely outshone by the women's in some kibbutzim.

Visitors from outside may be struck by the fact that lipstick is not used in the kibbutz. This is another matter which has its roots in the early days, when there was simply not enough money for cosmetics. It was, however, a luxury which, along with other urban customs, was given up with pioneering joy, for although the financial improvements would have long ago permitted its reintroduction, this was not done, not even in the wealthiest kibbutzim. As to jewelry, apart from a very occasional simple item, it is not worn, although no doubt available privately in many cases. Not only because its use on any appreciable scale would go against kibbutz ideals of material equality; in the kibbutz atmosphere, it would be felt as an artificial intrusion from a world whose values are more vain.

Many kibbutz customs are in essence symbolic, so that what is felt to be the true kibbutz spirit is never lost sight of; and extreme discretion in adornment is undoubtedly a manifestation of this attitude. Once a woman has adopted the kibbutz outlook, she will gain infinitely more satisfaction from being her natural self. She knows that she can live more happily if she is uninhibited by empty social conventions, and does not run after the much-vaunted but mostly worthless allurements of the outside world. The kibbutz woman can always afford to be sincere and forthright; and if she still has her problems, their solution will be found in that cooperative spirit and setting which her sister outside cannot enjoy. Her past has been invigorating if not wholly satisfying in some respects; her future promises unequaled brightness.

6

Recruitment and Absorption

Having considered the impact of the kibbutz on its members, it is natural to inquire how the members are selected, for nothing is of greater importance from the kibbutz point of view. It is desirable to avoid at all costs Robert Owen's idealistic mistake of taking in everyone who applied and thereby sowing the seeds of the early disruption of his experimental communalistic colonies of over a century ago. The system chosen was not original. It was, in fact, quite obvious; it consists of letting applicants serve a trial period before being accepted. This trial period is divided into two parts: for a minimum of half a year, the newcomer is granted the status of a guest only then, if approved by simple majority of the general meeting, he becomes a candidate for at least another half a year as a rule. Finally, by at least a two-thirds majority of either all the members, or all the members present at the meeting, he can be accepted as a new member of the kibbutz.

The candidate does not apply directly, but rather is considered by the absorption committee, one or more of whose members discuss with him his work and prospects, his background, and his approach to the general social atmosphere of the kibbutz. Afterwards, the entire committee will discuss the candidate and decide whether or not to recommend to the secretariat his promotion to full membership. The secretariat, in its turn, makes its recommendation, positive or negative, to the general meeting. The applicant thus has nothing to say, except to those of the absorption committee with whom he speaks initially, and he is certainly not allowed to attend any meeting discussing him. This may seem to leave him entirely in the power of the kibbutz, but there is no alternative. The kibbutz is an integral, organic body, and it cannot be too careful in the matter of accepting new members. Although great care is taken in the very full discussions, it is not only possible but even inevitable that mistakes are made from time to time and someone is accepted who turns out to be of dubious value to the kibbutz, or that a candidate who would eventually have been a definite asset is turned away. Considering, however, the very ample time that is given for experimentation, mistakes are not made too often. Once a decision is arrived at, there is no appeal. The head office of the kibbutz federation will certainly not interfere in a matter which is regarded as purely local. Each individual kibbutz must have total autonomy in the composition of its membership, except in the very rare instances where an ideological rift appears among existing members. In such a case the head office will decide who is in the wrong and will, if necessary, approve or veto a kibbutz decision that certain members must leave. Expulsion, however, is exceedingly rare, and can occur only if a member commits a grave social misdemeanor, or cannot continue in the ideological line of the kibbutz. Admission, on the other hand, is an everyday matter, but is equally serious and cannot be dealt with in an offhand manner. Kibbutz membership is normally for life, although a very small number of withdrawals do occur for personal reasons.

As a matter of fact, occasional complaints are heard that applications for membership in a kibbutz are, in spite of everything, handled improperly. It is said that the general meeting may reject an applicant for insufficient reasons, such as his personal style or even appearance, and that the members invent all kinds of rationalizations in their remarks or comments in order to justify their attitude. This may be true, and if so, may not be really a bad thing. If a large proportion of kibbutz membership feels in any way psychologically uncomfortable with a prospective member, it is probably to the good of all that the matter be decided negatively, however trivial the statement of the position might appear. While matters of psychology are often, if not usually, intangible, they are rarely altogether trivial. Nor must it be forgotten that the close personal relationship of kibbutz members is very much a matter of mutual reactions of personalities, a field in which dogmatism is especially dangerous.

It may appear that acceptance as a kibbutz member is an extremely difficult matter altogether. This, however, would be an exaggeration in most cases. The first and foremost requisite is that the applicant be suitable; and even those with the best will in the world are not always found suitable from the viewpoint of the kibbutz. Whether the kibbutz is right or wrong is secondary; the point of view of the kibbutz must prevail, or the entire delicate adjustment of the social unit which is the kibbutz would be threatened by tensions and personality stresses.

Suitability is to be regarded from two aspects: suitability for work and suitability for integration into the particular kibbutz concerned. In connection with the work, age is obviously an important factor. In general, anyone over thirty years of age will have more difficulty in getting accepted, if only because he will not have so many income-producing years before him to justify the kibbutz caring for him in his old age, quite apart from the question of supporting his family, if any. Kibbutzim always begin as youth groups, if for no other reason than because only strong young people can do the heavy physical work and live the hard life required during the first few years.

The best way to join a kibbutz is to join one of the training organizations in one's teens. But it is by no means the only way, and it is perfectly possible for the ordinary adult to join at a later stage—later, that is, both in his own life and in that of the kibbutz. If he has previous agricultural experience, or a useful technical skill in other fields, such as light industry, carpentry, metalworking, and water installations, he may be able to join easily; and he will be in a particularly good position if he is an electrician, driver, or motor mechanic. An unspecialized worker, especially if his background is in nonmanual labor, obviously cannot be so favorably received, but if he shows himself a willing worker in one of the needed branches, and if those in the kibbutz have enough patience to train him, he can quite possibly prove a success.

Women applicants are not generally expected to be specialists, although agricultural experience is a worthwhile background recommendation. In view of the need for household-service workers, and the general shortage of women in the kibbutzim, the ordinary woman has an easier chance of acceptance than the ordinary man.

The other side of the matter—that of suitability from the social-psychological point of view of the kibbutz—cannot be described accurately since it is mainly subjective and involves so many intangibles that every case must be dealt with individually on its merits. Educational background is taken into account to a much lesser extent than might be expected from the generally high cultural standards of the kibbutz. The primary reason for this seems to be a fear of the academic type who might not be able to undertake the practicalities of kibbutz life. Personality, therefore, is accorded a greater importance, and someone who is regarded as having a pleasing character will be accepted, regardless of a meager education. In practice, not many people of small education turn to the kibbutz in any case, so that there is no risk of a general lowering of its cultural standards on this account. It is a great advantage for an applicant to be a good mixer, and in practice the bright and breezy type, even if somewhat self-assertive, is preferred. There are, of course, limits to the acceptability of such tendencies, and any extremely bumptious or aggressive individual could not for a moment be seriously considered for membership. On the other hand, an extremely unassuming, meek, and mild type may also find it difficult to get accepted permanently.

The assortment of personality types found in almost any kibbutz today is such that it makes one wonder how some of the more awkward ones ever were accepted. A multitude of special reasons is responsible for this. The little woman who is good with the children but who has never managed to learn Hebrew and never will be able to cooperate in kibbutz functions or hold committee office was a victim of Hitler's and escaped miraculously at the last moment; in addition, she is a distant relative or friend of an oldtime member. The oddly aggressive orchard worker, who really is difficult to work with and who has caused trouble by his ill-judged handling of his companions, is expert in his field and was a renowned leader in the War of Liberation. The semi-invalid middle-aged man was involved in a tractor accident as an energetic young member of the founding youth group, and so on.

A very important consideration is that kibbutz membership grows infinitely more by the absorption of entire youth groups, even decades after a kibbutz's foundation, than by that of individuals. Although every youth group member can be, and at least to some extent always is considered separately, the group, as far as possible, will be accepted *en bloc*. This means that a borderline case can slip by in this manner, although he would stand little or no chance of acceptance were he judged by himself.

Yet another point is that a relatively easy way of joining a kibbutz is to marry into it. Marriage to a member does not of itself guarantee admission, but it obviously goes a long way towards it. If the member is a valued personality, only a very untoward spouse would be rejected by the kibbutz, which thus would lose the original member as well.

It is possible to buy membership in a kibbutz by becoming its benefactor and building a small house in it which will eventually revert to the use of the kibbutz itself. This road to the kibbutz is taken especially by older people who have children or other relatives in it, but such cases are extremely rare—regrettably so from the point of view of some kibbutzim. The membership of such a person would be, of course, rather nominal in character, apart from some exceptional cases. It is akin to the arrangement by which a member's aged parents may live in "parents' houses," enjoying the company of their children, to say nothing of their grandchildren, and receiving special diet as necessary, including such things as kosher meals in a nonreligious kibbutz. Kibbutz members know how to honor their parents, however differently they may have grown up from them, and how to accord every attention that love and respect dictate.

Such are the exceptions to be found in many a kibbutz population, to mention but a few examples, some relatively common, some extremely rare. But they undoubtedly are exceptions. For regular acceptance, the applicant need but be a normal, cheerful, agreeable person, preferably with a background in a manual trade, and in these days of rapid kibbutz development and acute shortage of manpower, let alone womanpower, he or she will undoubtedly be considered with the utmost goodwill, although hardly welcomed with open arms, for that is not the kibbutz way.

There are differences as to the readiness to accept new members in the different kibbutz federations. Apart from the religious federation, which requires a sincere orthodox background, no special characteristics are insisted upon. However, the case of Hakibbutz Haartzi is particularly interesting on account of its collective ideology (to be discussed later) and the intensity of its internal educational program in the principles of the movement. The latter has given rise to a degree of intensity in its pure kibbutzism, which results in an unusually high level of conscious selectivity where consideration of new members is concerned. Hakibbutz Hameuhad has the reputation of accepting applicants somewhat more freely. As to the Ihud haKvutzot vchaKibbutzim, no special outlook at all is usually attributed to it as far as its admissions policy is concerned.

In each case, the membership department at the federation head office can advise newcomers as to which kibbutzim they should turn with the best chances of being admitted, taking into account their background and preferences. The vital Israeli process of integrating immigrants from all the lands of the Jewish dispersion is one thing; the kibbutz rule to refer applicants to kibbutzim where a large proportion of the membership comes from the same country of origin, is another. The psychological difficulties of successful absorption are such that it is not normally worthwhile to add to them by bringing wide differences of national habits into the picture. With a full knowledge of Hebrew, it is quite practicable for a South African to settle happily in a mainly Rumanian, Hungarian, Bulgarian, or Polish kibbutz; but his totally different background would not make matters any smoother for the newcomer, who would make quicker and surer progress in an Anglo-Saxon kibbutz or one partly so.

Many kibbutzim have nevertheless been deliberately composed of highly contrasting elements put together quite abruptly, such as groups from Poland and the United States, or England and Hungary. The experiment, proceeding somewhat awkwardly at the start, has later succeeded brilliantly, so that after a few years, no one bothers to remember from which country his friend came; the provenance is no longer of the least practical importance.

But what can be done with groups of roughly equal size, cannot always be done so effectively with an individual, who is all too likely to be the odd man out. Where, however, the newcomer is himself one of even a small group, much more is possible in all respects. The members of the new immigrant group will give one another moral support, and the kibbutz will find it worthwhile to take the trouble to make all necessary special

provisions for them, justifying, for instance, the alloca-
tion of a teacher for Hebrew, since the group in effect constitutes a class of students, and so on. This is not to say that
every assistance is not given to an individual newcomer;
but obviously a group commands more respect and attention and can be more economically handled.

There are some kibbutzim which will make a guest a
candidate without too much discussion, the subsequent
final step to full membership being regarded as the significant one. Others appoint a guest to be a candidate only
after exhaustive examination of his position vis-à-vis the
kibbutz; in these kibbutzim once one is a candidate, one is
almost a member, and short of any unexpected difficulty,
full membership is almost automatic after the necessary
further period has elapsed. There is no difference in the
treatment accorded to guests or candidates or full members, except that the rights to speak and vote in meetings
are reserved for members. Guests may be allowed to attend
general meetings, at any rate after they have been in the
kibbutz for some time and show signs of wanting to become
permanent, and certainly candidates are expected to, in order that they become acquainted with the affairs of their
future kibbutz. Guests and candidates will naturally
have the simplest housing, perhaps in a very elementary
hut, perhaps in quite a good one. The best accommodation for newcomers is to be found in the younger kibbutzim, where one does not find such primitive shelters as
were used in the past and which still survive in odd corners of many of the older kibbutzim. The kibbutz rule of
equality extends also to them: food, clothing, repairs,
work, and holidays are the same as for full members.

Housing, in general, is a matter of seniority; well-built,
permanent rooms are allocated to members as a rule on a

point system of priority. Points are granted not only for the length of membership in the kibbutz, but also for age, imperfect health, and so on; seniority, however, is the most important factor by far. In this connection, it is interesting to observe that, by general agreement, a person who moves from one kibbutz to another, until he finds a permanent place (there is nothing to prevent anyone from doing this), can count his entire period of residence in the various kibbutzim, even if they belong to different federations, for purposes of calculating his seniority. For this purpose, the kibbutz movement as a whole stands as a unit. It is a pleasant point to reflect upon; but as there are many old members in kibbutzim who have had to wait twenty years or so for really good modern housing, such a system for figuring may not be worth much in practice. Good furniture, incidentally, is included in the term "housing" in regard to most of these considerations, but a minimum of simple furnishing is always available, even if stools have remained to this day more common than chairs.

As long as a newcomer is a guest or candidate, his personal possessions remain his own; upon admission as member, he is required to hand over to the kibbutz everything except purely personal belongings, which term is, however, very elastic nowadays. The time is long past when it was felt that it amounted to something like treason not to hand over every book and article of clothing to the common pool. Phonograph records and books still go into the general kibbutz collection and thereby enrich the communal library and the lives of all the members. But matters are not carried to extremes, since experience has shown that a degree of personal consideration, far from threatening kibbutz solidarity, actually adds to satisfaction, stability, and interest all round. Since a kibbutz member is legally a partner in a limited liability cooperative society, upon admission he must sign an undertaking rendering him personally liable for a nominal part of the debts incurred by the kibbutz. This, however, is merely a legal formality since the kibbutz itself is in turn a part of an economically powerful federation and is thus in no danger whatsoever of going bankrupt.

Should an applicant be rejected by the general meeting of the kibbutz, it may be difficult for him to get to know the reasons for his exclusion. Not unnaturally, the kibbutz is inclined to view its reasons as privy to itself; and a general phrase of "unsuitability" is about as much as the applicant is likely to hear from the kibbutz secretary when officially notified of the results. At the same time, it is important for a rejected applicant to know, as far as possible, what has made him appear unsuitable to the kibbutz, and especially so if he intends to try again in another kibbutz. His best course is to consult the most friendly of his contacts among the members, if possible the member on the absorption committee detailed to deal with him, and the tacts among the members, if possible, the member on the absorption committee detailed to deal with him. This member, using the requisite discretion, will usually intimate to him enough of the reasons to serve as guidance for the future. In many cases, however, the matter is a delicate one; the kibbutz itself may have done a great deal of rationalization and not revealed in open discussion the real reasons for rejection. In other cases, however, the matter may be quite simple, and there may be no reason whatsoever to make a secret of it. It can be a question of age or strength; or the applicant may be married and have children for whom there might be no room in the existing children's houses.

A single person is generally in a much better position to be admitted, as he causes far fewer complications for the kibbutz. On the other hand, there are kibbutzim which are not keen on accepting unmarried people, fearing that they may not make really stable members. Such practical considerations are, of course, usually gone into at the time of the original application to be accepted as a guest; if there is any doubt about him, the applicant may well be invited to come to work for a few days or weeks, after which, if he appears more or less appropriate and if suitable arrangements can be made in accordance with his requirements, he will be approved for full "guesthood." Generally the kibbutz secretariat, or the secretary himself, can take in a newcomer without promising anything officially; but if a guest is to stay more than a week or two, the general meeting must approve the secretarial suggestion. Similarly, unless the guest himself wishes to leave, which he is naturally free to do at any time, only the general meeting can pass a resolution as to his ouster.

From both the sociological and the immediately practical points of view, it would be interesting to know what motives direct a person towards the kibbutz as a way of life if he has not been born in it. There can be negative reasons —failure in and dissatisfaction with the everyday world— and positive ones—Zionist idealism, a desire for progressive social experimentation—or a mixture of both along with such motivations as having friends or relatives in a kibbutz. The important question is: Which are the motives that augur well for success as far as the permanent stability of the individual in the kibbutz is concerned? It may be worthwhile to ascertain, by means of a questionnaire, what is the range of motivations actually found among kibbutz members. The question would have to take in, in addition to motives, the life history of each member, his previous work, attitudes, education, hobbies, and other special interests. It would be of significance to know if there are, in general, significant differences between native Israelis and immigrants, between men and women, between those born in a kibbutz and those entering from outside at different ages, and so on. Such an inquiry may provide a valuable guide to the entire matter of future recruitment to the kibbutz. In addition, such a scholarly inquiry into the bases of kibbutz strength would be extremely valuable generally for a baffled humanity in search of new and more satisfactory social forms inherent in cooperative communities.

The sources of recruitment for the kibbutzim have changed very greatly since the days when the youth groups from Eastern Europe, inspired by new ideals, laid the foundations of the kibbutz movement. Undaunted by the grim and occasionally tragic experiences of those first hard years, the kibbutz has done more to redeem the Land of Israel for all the Jews who live there now and who will do so in the future than any other human factor in settlement. Immigration from Eastern Europe has long been reduced to less than a trickle, and only if it opened up on a large scale again could it again help the kibbutzim appreciably. Immigration is very slight from the countries of Western Europe and North America as well, and until there is a much greater realization in them of the significance of practical kibbutzism, they cannot yield much of the needed new blood. As to the Jewries in most of the Asian lands, and especially those in the Middle East, they have either been liquidated or reduced drastically, so that they too have practically dried up as sources of immigration. This leaves only North Africa, and to a much lesser extent, South Africa and South America, as potential reservoirs of kibbutzic immigration.

Even here, however, there are queries and problems. South African Jewry, although important and active in Zionism, has a limited appreciation of kibbutzism in practice. North African Jewry, although at present the main source of general immigration into Israel, has a tradition-bound individualist-family outlook, suffers from a lack of appropriate youth movements and progressive social education, and is, therefore, largely unsuited for kibbutz immigration. The Latin-American countries are now the leaders in supplying human material of excellent quality to the kibbutzim, and many young and older kibbutzim owe their successful development to immigrant groups from Mexico, Argentina, Brazil, Chile, Uruguay, as well as occasional individual members from other Latin-American countries.

Latin-American immigration appears to be based on the realization by Jewish parents that their children are destined to be submerged by the Catholic religious and social framework of these countries unless they strengthen their Jewish roots in the Jews' own land. Consequently, a relatively high proportion of the parents themselves emigrate to Israel with their children, or soon after them. The danger of assimilation may be particularly great in these countries, but it would be well to realize that it is not much smaller elsewhere. It has been suggested, for instance, that Jewry in England may hardly continue to exist in the next century, owing to the intermarriage rate, which is far from being exceptionally high.

Western Jewries in general simply must pay more attention to this matter in the future. They must become aware of the fact that the kibbutz is not only the most advanced form of Jewish life ever devised but a unique achievement in social organization generally. Although it is natural to think in Jewish terms where the kibbutz is concerned, the fact remains that in certain cases non-Jewish sympathizers have been successfully absorbed into it. There is not the least reason why this process should not continue and perhaps be greatly extended in the future. While an intensively religious Christian would doubtless feel uncomfortable in the Jewish environment, among the masses of the religiously indifferent majority in the modern Western world there may be a few who, recognizing the special social contribution to humanity of the kibbutz, might achieve creative satisfaction by identifying themselves with this, the world's most completely successful experiment in conscious democratic planning.

An obvious source of kibbutz recruitment close at hand is the youth of Israel itself. The appropriate organizations, through youth clubs, camps, tours, and similar spare-time training programs, are active all the time and send a steady stream to the kibbutzim each year. There is, however, need for ever greater extension of this work, and, strange as it appears, for more publicity in order to gain general public sympathy—this in Israel itself! For the peculiar situation is that the kibbutzim are at one and the same time both taken for granted and ignored among those sections of the population which have no direct contact with them. This, in spite of the fact that the kibbutz is, as it has always been, the basis of Israel's frontier fortifications, and the supplier of so much of the towns' food.

There is at least one small way in which the kibbutzim are able directly to attract town youngsters. Kibbutz education is on so high a level that some urban parents are willing to send their children to the regional kibbutz high schools where they are known as "outside children." They are, of course, not treated in any "outside" manner, and, under the influence of the kibbutz atmosphere, many of them freely decide to become kibbutz members themselves as they grow up. From quite a different angle, and without any direct reference to recruitment, the Ihud Hakvutzot Vehakibbutzim has worked out a scheme whereby certain of their kibbutzim are to become regional cultural centers, offering group study facilities, amateur theater and concert performances, and other cultural attractions to neighboring private villages. A private village, organized on the basis of the individual-enterprise system, could, of course, never develop similar cultural activities on its own. If this attractive project can be realized, it might well be that it would influence some of the young people in the private villages to join the local kibbutz.

There is another possibility which, however, has not yet been tried. From time to time considerable numbers of workers are hired by the kibbutzim, mostly in building work which the kibbutz members cannot carry out for themselves. The suggestion is that a special status of guest-membership for these hired workers be created, so that they might share in many of the services of the kibbutz such as food, clothing, and education for their children. The result would be that they would become something like outside members, spending only their days in the kibbutz, but gradually becoming more and more integrated. The scheme, however, would have to be extremely flexible, as some jobs last for only a short time. It would therefore seem essential to draw up a schedule for the conversion into monetary terms of all the services the kibbutz can render to such temporary workers. If the hired worker does not elect to make use of the services, he could be paid instead. This is simply an extension of the practice of paying for meals, already common. Naturally, the essence of the scheme would lie in a subsidization of the services provided, so that it would pay the worker to utilize the kibbutz services to the greatest possible extent. For the kibbutz this would also be advantageous due to the economies of its collectivization. The main reason why workers stay outside the kibbutz is the ubiquitous hope of the immigrant to make good on his own and to have his own home and, possibly, piece of land. But the kibbutz is in the unique position of being able to offer a much quicker way of making good and attaining personal independence in association with others. Possibly, the lessons of self-controlled individuality in the coordinated classless democracy which is the kibbutz have to be preceded by a little social bribery before they can be taught. It may be too much to expect the untutored outsider to take the kibbutz path without practical incentive. Any such scheme would have to be tried out on a small scale at first, and if it failed to yield satisfactory results after a reasonable test, it would then have to be given up.

An obvious reason why recruitment to the kibbutzim is smaller than would be desirable is that among people coming from the modern Western world only a minority likes rural life. The majority is reluctant even to try kibbutz life, although the rural aspect of the kibbutz community is a very different thing from usual village life.

This brings us to the question of whether urban kibbutzim are a practical possibility. One such experiment was carried out on the outskirts of Tel Aviv in recent years. It was called Kibbutz Efal. Its members lived a kibbutsic life in a building of their own. But they could not agree about the pooling of incomes earned in their various urban employments. Those who earned more felt they were being penalized by those who earned less. This resulted in a breakup and a return to individualism. Although in a rural kibbutz too the cash value of work done in various branches of the economy has a wide range, the differences are not felt, since generally no actual money is handled, and what appears in the accounts at the end of the quarter remains on paper without exciting individualist passions.

It is indeed a serious question whether this difficulty in urban kibbutzim can be overcome. Some regard the entire matter as hopeless since without land and the consequent attachment to the soil, kibbutz members cannot achieve that level of loyalty to their community which is immediately and only possible in a rural environment. Others feel that a solution could be found if the members of the urban kibbutz all worked in a joint cooperative enterprise, equivalent to the rural kibbutz farm, after the manner of the French "Communities of Work." As among the latter, communal life could center on the cooperative factories or workshops, and the members could retain their private homes with the most intensive liaison possible among them. This would be an interesting and valuable experiment, but would fall short of actual kibbutzism. It would certainly seem a pity if the kibbutz movement felt it impossible to make further attempts to transplant its remarkable social achievements from the rural to an urban setting.

Meanwhile, there are one or two groups of young people in England, for example, who pool their diverse city earnings and live communally in an urban house, while waiting to embark upon their agricultural training and to emigrate to Israel. Once in Israel, they plan to become kibbutz members. There seems to be no reason why this kind of effort should not be expanded, so that more and more people could be self-trained in kibbutzic living while still town dwellers. In this manner stable urban kibbutzim might become possible.

The abortive Kibbutz Efal was a visionary enterprise of Hakibbutz Hameuhad. Perhaps the vision should be extended to cover a larger number of urban kibbutzim. Then the rural and urban kibbutzim could lend one another added strength and provide practical facilities, such as rural holidays for the town children or assistance in purchasing the town-manufactured requirements of the rural kibbutzim. In this way entirely new and much wider horizons would open up, and a much greater percentage of the population could be absorbed within the social orbit of kibbutz democracy.

But even if recruitment to kibbutzim from outside resources never again reaches the level that it did during the Hitler persecution in Europe, the future of the kibbutzim would still not be in jeopardy. They could, in fact, maintain themselves at their present level through their natural increase without any outside recruitment. In fact, old, established kibbutzim with populations around five hundred are making plans to accommodate within a very few decades populations double that size. The present and future children of the kibbutzim will, of course, also create new kibbutzim in every part of the land in the years ahead.

The pressing problem, though, is how to get through the next few years while the kibbutzim carry out the big development schemes which they have undertaken. This is a natural phenomenon connected with a certain phase of growth. Some say that the present kibbutz members are overambitious collectively and have bitten off more than they can chew, but such a charge is unfair, for the plain economic fact is that a farm and its associated enterprises can be conducted either on a small or on a large scale; it is precisely the intermediate size which is beset by all sorts of operating difficulties. To get economically established on a large scale is therefore the essence of current kibbutz effort, and no time is consequently more valuable than the present for securing help from outside.

However, the kibbutzim cannot afford to lower their standards by lowering their admission requirements, for this would merely lead to future decay instead of assured progress. The foregoing review of the problems of recruitment, both from the standpoint of the individual applicant and from that of the kibbutzim, therefore, touches upon what is at present the most vital issue of the entire kibbutz movement.

While it has been possible to say a good deal about recruitment, the related and very essential further process, that of the absorption of the newcomer, must be dealt with much more summarily. Absorption is surrounded by numerous psychological intangibles which, in the present stage of our knowledge, can, in many cases, be only sensed rather than clearly expressed, let alone analyzed. Nevertheless, some general remarks are possible.

First of all it should be emphasized that absorption is largely an unconscious process. However much the newcomer thinks he understands the atmosphere of the kibbutz, it is virtually certain that he is a very long way from truly grasping its spirit. The spirit of the kibbutz is, to a very large extent, a matter of indefinable attitude which grows on one with time but which cannot possibly be learned from books, lectures, or even personal conversation with a helpful oldtimer who knows it but cannot explain it. At the same time it is also a matter of interpersonal relations, which makes each kibbutz slightly different, according to the main individual types found in it. And, it is also a matter of getting attuned. He who can feel his way most rapidly and correctly is absorbed most quickly within the kibbutz framework.

It is, of course, advisable for a newcomer to learn as much as possible about the objective facts of kibbutz living, to put himself in a deliberately receptive frame of mind, to let the kibbutz be always right, however odd some of its dealings with him or in general may seem to him, and to give full expression to his personal interests only after he has become well established. One does well to remember that it is virtually impossible afterwards to efface the psychological effects of a serious clash of opinion near the outset. This does not mean that one must render oneself a nonentity by negating one's own characteristics during the preliminary period; on the contrary, an exaggerated effect of giving oneself up wholly to the kibbutz would produce an unfavorable impression. But any kind of "crankiness," in whatever direction, is to be avoided at all costs, and perhaps even any too marked specialization of interest, for such things are apt to arouse the suspicion that the newcomer cannot become a devoted member of the kibbutz in the future. It is the middle course that should be pursued instead. If an applicant shows, during his trial period, that he has a lively mind, the kibbutz is the more likely to regard him as a person who may, in due time, contribute to its collective life. Practical personal problems, such as family affairs or work matters, can be discussed objectively with a member of the absorption committee, and do not give rise to so much doubt.

It is probably easier for an immigrant to adjust to Israeli kibbutz life than it is for the native Israeli who has had a previous home in the same land. The local person has home ties and a consequent home pull only a few hours' journey away; for him it is sometimes extremely difficult to make the effort of adjustment. He may have a long internal struggle before he can feel that the kibbutz, and not his previous address, is his true home. The practical aspects of the matter are naturally much easier for him; he is at home with the language, the customs of the land, the food, the climate, and other factors.

The immigrant must relegate his foreign past to the museum of his mind and start with a clean slate, so to speak. In some cases, of course, the strangeness of the new ways may prove too much for him too. He may be unable to go through the absorption process successfully unless given skilled and sympathetic personal help which, with the best will in the world, not every kibbutz can always supply. For the native Israeli, however, it is easier to retreat to his previous home if he comes up against difficulties. And since his home is not very far away and to return to it does not involve the serious matter of re-emigration, he will more readily choose this course. In the case of the many youth groups drawn from among the children of relatively recent immigrants who are sent to the kibbutzim for periods of a few years, the parental pull is close at hand. The result is that a large proportion of them leave the kibbutz without ever considering membership. Unfortunately, there is often a solid economic reason for this: the parents need their children's earnings, and in the kibbutz there are no monetary rewards. As far as possible, the kibbutzim should try to arrange a modicum of financial support for the parents, but financial resources are so limited that, in general, little can be done in this way.

Both immigrants and native Israelis who have difficulty in feeling themselves at home in the kibbutz can move on to other forms of rural settlement, especially to moshavim in which the farm is worked collectively, exactly as in the kibbutz, but where the members live in private houses and manage their own households. But even such a shift evidences failure to absorb the kibbutz outlook, to appreciate its unique human values, and to take that decisive step forward into pure democracy which makes a person something larger than himself.

A vital aspect of absorption into the kibbutz community for an immigrant is learning Hebrew, for not even a kibbutz composed of a homogeneous ethnic group can countenance carrying on its affairs in any other but the language of the country. Otherwise, it would, in effect, be cut off from the rest of Israel, including its sister kibbutzim and its own federation. Newcomers in kibbutzim may have to resort to Yiddish, if they know it, as a temporary *lingua franca*, or use their native English, French, or whatever language it may be. One can always be sure to find at least a few members who know some European language sufficiently. But the sooner a working elementary knowledge of Hebrew is attained, the easier life in the kibbutz becomes.

Either private or group lessons are always arranged for the newcomers. But unless an immigrant has learned a great deal of Hebrew before arriving in the kibbutz, it is more than worthwhile for him to start with an intensive schedule of half a day of work and half a day of learning Hebrew (which his work pays for) for a period of at least five or six months, but preferably a year, before becoming a full-time worker-guest in the kibbutz of his choice. Since only a small number of kibbutzim run such intensive courses, his learning period may be carried out in a kibbutz which he would not choose to enter as a member. One cannot overemphasize the importance of learning Hebrew until a working knowledge is achieved. Until this is done, definite participation in kibbutz affairs cannot take place and absorption must necessarily be far from complete. Lack of a sufficient knowledge of Hebrew is likely to be a source of great frustration and prevent the newcomer from working out a successful adjustment. He will remain cut off from much of the life and interests of the older members, to say nothing of the culture of the country as a whole. Although this is generally recognized, an understanding kibbutz will not reject a candidate because of his insufficient knowledge of Hebrew alone; he will be given more time to master the language after his initial trial year if in other respects he satisfies the kibbutz that he will make a good member. The fact remains that, in the proper sense of the term, his absorption cannot be concluded until he does achieve that mastery. It is fortunate that, contrary to current belief in some quarters, Hebrew is not among the world's difficult languages; its fascinatingly logical structure and comparatively simple vocabulary render it eminently suitable to serve as the Israeli Esperanto in tying together the dispersed Jewish communities from the ends of the earth into a common culture. And, of course, no other language but the ancient tongue of the Bible could possibly have gained general acceptance in Israel.

In addition to Hebrew lessons, some kibbutzim arrange lecture courses in simple Hebrew for newcomers on the organization of the branches of the kibbutz, its history, and outlook. These lectures, if well done, can be of considerable help in the absorption process, although they are no substitute for personal guidance.

An interesting and very successful experiment on a large scale has been carried out by Hakibbutz Haartzi, including a residential seminar for several days, in which new members from many kibbutzim participated in an intensive study of the principles of the movement. Such a study gives a solid foundation to developing kibbutz outlook of the new member. He has the opportunity to raise queries and obtain definitive replies, as well as to meet new members from the other kibbutzim of the federation and to exchange opinions and discuss difficulties with them. The obvious advantages of this method are so clear that, no doubt, it will become regular practice in the future, and that increasing numbers of new members will be enabled by their kibbutzim to benefit by it. The essence of absorption in the kibbutz lies in the voluntary dedication of one's life to its aims and ideals, a dedication which, far from limiting the personality of the individual, sets it in a larger sphere, enriches it with a nobler purpose and, by making social democracy an intensive reality in its most immediate and purest sense, enables the individual to realize his full potentialities as a member of human society.

7

Collective Ideology

There is one aspect of the organization of Hakibbutz Haartzi (the kibbutz federation which is, by a narrow margin, the largest) which has given rise to a good deal of misunderstanding. It is the concept frequently and officially referred to as "Collective Ideology." Those who have not inquired into the matter sufficiently might easily misunderstand it and take it to mean some kind of thought control. What it *does* mean is that the members of this federation voluntarily accept the majority decision as to policy or political thought, and do not tolerate any organized opposition. The key words here are "voluntarily" and "organized." Any member who cannot voluntarily accept the policies arrived at after due democratic discussion in the movement is naturally always free to leave, but as it is rare for any established member to wish to uproot himself in this manner, he can remain without question as long as he does not organize opposition—that is, as long as he keeps his opinions to himself and so does not threaten the political solidarity of the membership. In practice, probably a large number of members have personal reservations about one policy or another, but since they agree on main principles (or else they would not have entered the feder-

112

ation in the first place), they do not usually think it worthwhile to quibble openly on small points. There are cases known of Hakibbutz Haartzi members who support a party other than Mapam (to which the federation is attached), to the extent of subscribing to the daily newspaper of another political party. At election times, the vote in most kibbutzim of Hakibbutz Haartzi is not one hundred per cent for Mapam, although some kibbutzim do, in fact, achieve this. Any member can vote for another party as long as he does not attempt to influence others; in any case, under the secret ballot, he cannot be identified if he does not wish to be.

Education in the Mapam political outlook is part of the absorption process of the new members who come from outside the party ranks. Anyone who definitely opposes this policy would not be likely to be accepted; nor would he, in such a case, apply to this particular federation. The Mapam policy of Hakibbutz Haartzi is a logical development of kibbutzism itself and fits it so well that it is not surprising that its kibbutzim are the core of the party's strength. There is, of course, a more general policy common with the other workers, both in town and country; there is the aim of infusing society with something of the spirit of the kibbutz by reorganizing, or at least influencing, it in the direction of cooperative enterprise; there is an attitude of friendliness towards all peoples, including the Arabs, in the hope of eventually winning them over to peaceful coexistence. These are ideals any adherent of kibbutz principles is ready to accept.

The matter can be further understood by taking a glance at the position prevailing, by contrast, in the other two major federations. The fourth one, the religious federation, obviously, has an orientation of its own, amounting to the most solid collective ideology of all and linked with the religious political bloc in the country. The contrast with Hakibbutz Hameuhad, linked with the Ahdut Avodah party, is not, in fact, very marked. The two federations differ in their attitude towards the Israeli Arabs, Hakibbutz Hameuhad being less friendly towards them. This difference was a cardinal point in the separate crystallization of the two federations.

The matter, however, was far from academic. Hakibbutz Haartzi, through the Mapam party, has organized pioneering youth groups in the Israeli Arab villages and towns, designed not to draw Arab youth into the kibbutzim (which would be the death of their own villages) nor even to persuade them to form kibbutzim of their own (which is regarded as premature) but to form cooperatives and bring fresh life to their own villages in their own way. To put it mildly, Jews take their politics seriously; but the practical side of this question is no less significant than the theoretical, since young Arab training groups are to be found from time to time in kibbutzim of Hakibbutz Haartzi, where they learn the latest farming methods, but they are not found in those of Hakibbutz Hameuhad. The latter federation, in addition, has a slightly different collective ideological outlook, characterized by a somewhat looser party allegiance.

The position in the Ihud Hakvutzot Vehakibbutzim federation is entirely different. Here one finds definite opposition to the idea of collective ideology. In practice, the vast majority of members support, and vote for, the Mapai party, but the relationship with the party, instead of being intimate, is remote and uncertain. The Ihud kibbutzim cannot get party support for their demands for cheap credit and other such essentials. The party, in general, appears to regard its associated kibbutzim very remotely, unable to make up its mind whether they are liabilities or assets.

As to the Ihud kibbutzim themselves, there does not seem to be in them that full measure of solidarity which a vigorous, shared political outlook gives. No kibbutz lives unto itself: in this respect, it is quite unlike the isolated monastery of past ages. But the degree to which it participates in the affairs of the outside world is dictated by the political outlook it embraces. If its members have vigorous and disparate political orientations, the intimate communal life will be broken up by dissension; if they are politically lukewarm, they do not carry the pure democracy of the kibbutz to its conclusion. The kibbutz is a cooperative socio-moral force, and the complete democrat cannot logically refrain from wishing to bring this force to bear upon the world in general. The only fully satisfactory solution, therefore, is for kibbutz members to follow an active policy in unison, and this is precisely collective ideology.

A difficult economic and moral problem for the kibbutz is the question of hired labor. As has been previously mentioned, outside workers are from time to time hired by the kibbutzim, primarily in construction work. The principle formulated by the purest kibbutzists to meet this contingency is that hired labor can legitimately be used for the construction of capital goods, such as houses, water installations, farm buildings, and so on, but not for the production of consumer goods designed for outside markets.

The reason for the distinction is simple: the kibbutz lives by making a profit on its marketed produce; if it employs hired labor and makes a profit on their work, it is exploiting them. If there was no profit in employing the workers, they would not be employed; if they are employed, the resultant profit, according to kibbutz principles, rightly belongs to them, for under kibbutz morality no man has a right to make a profit from another's work.

The plea that the employer provides the essential capital equipment without which the worker could not accomplish anything, and can therefore legitimately receive payment for it in the form of profit, is not valid within the framework of the kibbutz outlook. Kibbutz members built up their capital equipment as they went along (at the cost of a low standard of living). Any worker can do likewise by means of cooperative schemes. He can join some form of cooperative village or cooperative urban organization in industry or other field. From the pure kibbutz point of view, therefore, exploiting a worker is prohibited for kibbutz members cannot allow themselves to add to their amenities of life by profiting from the work of others. But if all resultant profits are paid back to the worker in higher wages, there is no sense in employing him at all.

It may be suggested that there is a value in utilizing the unemployed to increase food and other production. Unfortunately, this is impracticable for the simple reason that if the kibbutzim offered higher wages than were paid elsewhere, the workers of the country would flock to the kibbutzim, the whole economic structure of the country would be affected, and the kibbutzim could not possibly deal with the problems involved—they would clearly be swamped by outsiders. Moreover, the existence of a general labor market in the country forbids any such generous experiments. Consequently, there is the unhappy paradox of unemployed workers outside, and an intense shortage of labor power within the kibbutzim.

These difficulties do not apply in the case of constructing capital goods. These are not sold at a profit upon completion. The houses, installations, and so on, are used on the spot, for the duration of their lifetime, by the members themselves. A rigid purist might object that, even so, they are part of the profit picture, since profits could not be made at all if there were no farm buildings and equipment, to say nothing of houses for the members and their children to live in while carrying on their cooperative production. While true enough in an abstract way, the matter is very indirect and bears no comparison with the direct employment of workers for the purpose of additional profits on marketable farm crops and industrial products. To extend the principle so ridiculously far would be to carry logic to an absurd end. This is not the way kibbutz members, who have hammered out their policies during decades of hard experience, think or act.

The attitude displayed on this issue by the different federations is very illuminating. Hakibbutz Haartzi always knew where it must logically stand. In a few cases, individual kibbutzim shortsightedly succumbed to the commercial temptation of employing outside workers in order to take advantage of market conditions or, somewhat less culpably, to advance some development scheme. When this happened, the arbitration court of the movement took requisite steps to put an end to such procedures. More tardily, the same position was eventually arrived at by Hakibbutz Hameuhad. In the absence of regular kibbutzic collective ideology, the position of the Ihud

Hakvutzot Vehakibbutzim was more uncertain. Its associated parliamentary party, Mapai, had for long appealed to the kibbutzim to absorb the unemployed by engaging them at standard rates of pay. Consequently, hired labor became so common for everyday productive purposes that the federation's weekly magazine printed a letter from a kibbutz member to the effect that if the kibbutzim do not break the hired-labor system soon, it would break them. Hakibbutz Haartzi's weekly magazine was, of course, quick to reprint this comment as a frank justification of its own ideological standpoint!

It is important to realize the demoralizing effects hired labor can have in a kibbutz. There is an all too human tendency, from which kibbutz members are not exempt, to leave the hard work to hirelings and simply stand by and supervise. This, of course, totally negates the kibbutz spirit of honorable self-endeavor and imperils kibbutz morale as a whole.

Subsequently the Ihud Hakvutzot Vehakibbutzim formed outside companies for productive enterprise, in which the kibbutzim could participate but which, not being themselves kibbutzim or integral parts of kibbutzim, could freely employ hired workers. Although the purist might object that this was a morally unworthy way out of the dilemma, this type of solution will have to be countenanced as long as it does not impair true kibbutzism at home. Even Hakibbutz Haartzi, for instance, has an interest in a pottery factory in which nowadays only the managers are kibbutz members, the workers themselves mostly coming from the outside.

Such is the application of collective ideology in practice. A kibbutz member who did not accept the logic of this attitude would either have to keep very quiet about his opinions or else make other arrangements. An adequate realization of what true kibbutzism stands for makes it easy to accept norms, standards, and rules which have been arrived at democratically over the years before becoming final conclusions, or were formulated in the early days of the movement by its elected leaders and amply justified by the experience of subsequent years.

The Polish Jewish youth movement which later became the core of Hakibbutz Haartzi established firmly in its earliest years that its strength lay in its collective ideology. Although in the course of time associated groups did break away from it, the fact remains that the whole history of this federation is a clear example of the adage that unity is strength.

No little interest attaches to a phenomenon like this from the standpoint of democracy in general, for no democratic system can be strong if the people living under it are disunited in outlook. In the modern national political democracies differences of opinion, sufficient for the formation of parliamentary oppositions, exist; but there can be no difference of opinion about the fundamentals of the organization of national life. In the American democracy, the Democratic and the Republican parties are both equally devoted to the American way of life and each calls for comparatively minor modifications in one direction or another. In the British democracy, it has long been observed that the Labor party has almost always shared the foreign policy of the Conservatives, and although it has its own stand on internal issues, it is united with the Conservatives in its opposition to any attack on the fundamentals of the British way of life.

In the small local and intensive democratic community of the kibbutz unity has to crystallize far more narrowly. In it, even a limited organized opposition would split the membership asunder. Collective ideology, therefore, far from being a stumbling block, is the logical outcome of kibbutz necessity.

8

Kibbutz Democracy and the Future

Although it is impossible not to praise most features of
the kibbutz, it would be unjustifiable to give the impression that it is perfect, or even the best that can be achieved.
Attention has been drawn to certain weaknesses, and it is
freely acknowledged that improvement is still called for.
The progressive development of the kibbutz movement,
starting as it did on a basis of little more than accidental
necessity, undoubtedly augurs well for the future. The
need, however, for continued effort is evident.

It has been pointed out by many observers, that a new
social form, even of the finest quality, runs the risk
of eventually rigidifying and thus losing its creative
vitality and the power of fully satisfying the human needs
of its members. The organization of the kibbutz is by no
means unduly complicated in view of the tasks it must
carry out. Nevertheless, it must guard against becoming
a form for form's sake. It must remain infused by
the spirit of purposeful realism. It must not overlook the
manifest shortcomings, such as inadequate attendance at
general meetings, or the very slight, but still conceivable
risks, such as the reduction of democratic values by the
kibbutz equivalent of demagogy in the form of speeches

121

made by brilliant but shallow-thinking members. It must attend to the unsolved problems, such as those of the women members, or its inability to establish urban kibbutzim.

A serious general criticism is sometimes heard, to the effect that kibbutz members are likely to develop a parochial outlook because of their relative isolation from the everyday affairs of the population as a whole and their preoccupation with the immediate concerns of their own village. This point is not difficult to refute, for the fact is that the kibbutzim regard themselves as an active and integral part of the workaday world around them and, as has been pointed out, make most effective showings in many national fields, notably the political and cultural ones. A certain percentage of kibbutz members undoubtedly can allow themselves to withdraw into parochialism—a danger to be guarded against. Yet even so, the social achievement of the kibbutzim towers head and shoulders above that of the incomplete democracy of the Western world in general. It goes far beyond all the improvements introduced by cooperative villages of various types in Israel and elsewhere. Only a very few small religious communities, actuated by a faith which can have but little appeal to most ordinary men, have achieved a superdemocracy which in some respects may exceed that of the kibbutz, but which must be regarded as impracticable as a form of life for large numbers of people. Even the kibbutz movement it not yet within immediate sight of its first 100,000; but it is firmly and broadly based and expanding continuously. Consequently, it is by no means an idle question to ask, in general terms, how far the kibbutz is likely to become a mass movement in the accepted sense of the term in the future, perhaps even outside, as well as within, its native land.

As has been stated previously, the growth of the kibbutz movement in Israel itself is assured by the natural increase of its own population, and by additions from the outside. Nevertheless, only in another two or three generations can it become a mass movement in relation to the total agricultural population of the country. Much depends on what influx the kibbutzim receive from the outside and what will happen to the private and cooperative villages, on whether they will retain their numerical predominance unchallenged or not. Owing to the strength of the individualist tradition of their devotees, it cannot be expected that they or their children will look towards kibbutzism to any measurable extent, even if their weaker economic organization causes their standard of living to decline in relation to that of the kibbutz.

What may well happen in the long run is that, in spite of all propaganda, private-village children will turn more and more to the towns (as has been the case in the Western world generally), whereas kibbutz children will remain loyal to their life and values, influenced by the democratic intensity of their background and training. It is therefore conceivable that the time will come, in the not very distant future, when the kibbutzim will prove the salvation of Israeli agriculture and rural living, just as they laid the foundations of the rural yishuv in the past. The type of village which holds its children is the type which will not only survive but become the basic or mass type in the future. The future rural Israel may well be one in which the large and prosperous villages will typically be kibbutzim, while the others will be smaller, more modest and socially less stable. But nothing would be more foolish and futile than to attempt to prophesy. There are far too many uncertain factors, both social and economic. The most that can be said is that he who takes an optimistic outlook on the kibbutz would seem to be more amply justified than the pessimist, whose forecasts are vitiated by this vigorously constructive social phenomenon.

The second part of the question, whether kibbutzism is suitable for export on a large scale, is more difficult to answer. A study group of the United Nations Food and Agriculture Organization, meeting in Tel Aviv in 1956, came to the conclusion that the kibbutz was the least exportable of Israel's different types of cooperative villages, simply because it was the most intensive one. It was emphasized that the uniform political outlook which alone can ensure success in communal life of this nature cannot normally be found among farming communities elsewhere.

This conclusion undoubtedly holds good in many, if not most cases. Particularly promising for the kibbutz would appear to be India. At least one small kibbutz already exists experimentally in that vast land; a representative from it visited Israel and was much impressed by a kibbutz of Hakibbutz Haartzi, from which he learned a great deal. The semicommunal structure and outlook of Indian villages does give a possible basis for kibbutzism to develop. That a mass kibbutz movement in India could redeem its rural population more rapidly and effectively from its present social backwardness than any less radical method is most likely. The question is, however, whether a sufficiency of local leaders will arise to render such a development practical. Nor is there any point in making vague remarks about still more remote possibilities in some other countries in spite of a definite beginning in the French Sahara.

One must be content to leave the matter open; but if enough enthusiasts could be found in countries outside Israel to undertake the building up of kibbutz communities on the sound ideological principles which have been described, successful results might well be achieved. Unfortunately, the socio-psychological study of most peoples in the modern world is not yet sufficiently advanced to make a reliable assessment of the practical potentialities of kibbutzism possible.

The mere fact that most people, without knowing anything about communal living, are inclined to reject it out of hand as soon as it is mentioned is greatly to be regretted. It is quite possible that many more than the one-twentieth of the present Jewish population of Israel which lives in kibbutzim could actually do so effectively and happily if they tried—but they do not try. It is for this reason that we must know much more about kibbutz mentality, if any such mentality exists; only after such knowledge is acquired can social planning include kibbutzim among the potential solutions to some of its problems. All that can be said at present on the issue is that the Israeli kibbutzim merit all the additional support they can obtain, although their future is assured in any case, whether it will actually be of mass dimensions or not. The example presented by the Israeli kibbutzim to the world at large is a challenge to which other peoples could well respond in their own best and long-range interests.

A last question remains: how much can Western democracy in general learn from the kibbutzim? While it is true that the full advantages of kibbutz life accrue only to those living it, it has certain aspects which deserve the utmost attention of modern democracies even if their outlook makes it impossible for them to consider practicing the kibbutz ideal. There is the true self-government of those who consider it a primary social duty to participate actively in local political affairs, which can serve as an example for local authorities everywhere. There is the kibbutz practice of periodic elections of officials which prevents the crystallization of fixed bureaucracies; this practice could well be utilized or adapted in other democratic bodies. The general meeting of the kibbutz could be emulated by placing greater emphasis on meetings of citizens to discuss municipal affairs, and on street and district groups.

Probably not more than this, if as much, can normally be transplanted from the kibbutz setting; it amounts to little more than the shadow of the complete democracy which reigns in the kibbutz itself. Yet even this could infuse Western democracy with some slight reflection of the grandeur of the democratic spirit which ancient Greece knew and which the kibbutzim in our time have made their own in such striking fashion. For, in its truest sense, democracy is not merely a social system—not even the best of social systems—but much more: the realization of the dignity of man expressed in social life with his neighbors.

That strange people, the Jews, a fossilized remnant of ancient Syriac civilization, as Toynbee called them, have, in the course of their incredible history, given many gifts of incomparable moral value to the world, although they themselves have no more lived up to their own highest principles than have any other people. In our own day they have suffered the most ghastly calamity that ever befell any people—the Hitlerite slaughter of six million of them,

*Kibbutz Yehi Am, seen from a Crusader castle (Courtesy of
Zionist Archives and Library)*

Kibbutz Kfar Gileadi, near the Syrian border (Courtesy of Zionist Archives and Library)

Kibbutz Ein Gev on the shores of Lake Kinneret, with Syrian mountains in the background (Courtesy of Zionist Archives and Library)

Kibbutz Yasur (Courtesy of Hakibbutz Haartzi)

Sdot Yam (Courtesy of Zionist Archives and Library)

Kiryat Amal, near Haifa (Courtesy of Zionist Archives and Library)

Kibbutz Ginegar (Courtesy of Zionist Archives and Library)

*Modern milking methods at Kibbutz Givat-Brenner, south
of Tel Aviv (Courtesy of Zionist Archives and Library)*

*A Kibbutz Sasa cowboy, near the Sea of Galilee (Courtesy
of Hakibbutz Haartzi)*

Kibbutz Givat-Brenner's work-assignment board (Courtesy of Zionist Archives and Library)

The communal dining-hall at Kibbutz Givat-Brenner (Courtesy of Zionist Archives and Library)

The evening meal at Kibbutz Shaar Hagolan (Courtesy of Hakibbutz Haartzi)

The Kibbutz Givat-Brenner orchestra (Courtesy of Zionist Archives and Library)

The swimming pool at Kibbutz Hazorea (Courtesy of Zionist Archives and Library)

Folk dance by Kibbutz Shaar Hagolan dancers at Kibbutz Sasa, with Mt. Adir in the background (Courtesy of Hakibbutz Haartzi)

the most gigantic crime in human history, before which all the massacres of the past fade into comparative insignificance. Yet, in the same period, they progressed as far as they could in perfecting their latest gift to the world— the kibbutz, a model of moral social organization, in which a man can attain his full human stature more easily than almost anywhere else. A world which acquiesced ungraciously to the return of this ancient people of its Biblical homeland where, in the upsurge of a national enthusiasm this gift was forged, has not yet appreciated its true value.

The more widely the theory and practice of the kibbutz is known, the more it will be valued; that is the reason for this book. As the first president of the State of Israel, the late Dr. Chaim Weizmann, stressed when he opened the first parliament which assembled after the declaration of independence, the ultimate justification for the existence of the reborn land is the message that will go forth from Zion in the future. Jewish nationalism is not, as with other nationalisms, its own justification: the People of the Book, who gave its basic vision to the Western world, cannot be content with a provincial outlook. In his innate passion for social justice, the Jew wants to see all humanity united in the bond of brotherhood of which Isaiah dreamed in his ancient prophecy. The kibbutz is an integral part of the modern message to go forth from Zion; it constitutes yet another sterling Jewish contribution towards the general good of mankind: a living model of the purest democracy in the world.

BOOK II

Go East, Young Man!

Diary of an English Emigrant's First Year in an
Israeli Kibbutz

Prologue

I had often wondered whether sighting the Land of Israel for the first time was really as romantic as some people had made it out to be. On the whole, I think it was. I got up at 5 A.M. the morning my ship was due to reach Tel Aviv at 7. It was still almost entirely dark and nothing definite could be seen, but at one point on the horizon there was a thickening of the darkness which might have denoted land. Half an hour later there was no real doubt about it as far as I was concerned, although a fellow-passenger said, "Clouds." It was quite light now, and those spiky lumps rising from a long ridge were fairly clearly low mountains. Soon afterwards, the sun rose quickly over them: the autumn sun rising from the east over Eretz Israel. My new land! Or my old one? Someone on board had said that he had been absent from Israel four months. My comment was that I had been absent two thousand years. Much more than the mountains to the north was visible now: a long, low stretch of coastline southwards had come into the picture. What would this unknown country hold for me? Behind that coastline were farms, towns, the desert. It was not only Israel. It was Asia, and

131

this was the first time I had set eyes on a continent other than Europe. As the ship covered the last few miles of the far end of the eastern Mediterranean and approached the shore of the Asiatic continent, a blur of whitish buildings began to take shape and Tel Avi–Jaffa became a personal reality for me.

But only to a minimum extent. My boat lay off Jaffa all day, discharging her cargo over the side to lighters and her passengers by launch. I eventually ascertained from the Israeli Customs Officers who came on board that immigrants with papers like mine for Haifa were not allowed to land for a day trip on shore. It was a particularly interesting moment when these officials arrived in their launch: the passengers greeted them with smiles and cries of "Shalom," both of which were warmly reciprocated. Never before have I seen such a friendly welcome given to Customs officials, and no doubt I never shall again. Nothing could have made it clearer to me that all Jews are brothers on returning to the land of their fathers. Incidentally, these Customs officers provided another novelty: they wore khaki shorts.

A glance at the men who came on board to help the crew to discharge cargo showed that Israeli living standards were considerably higher than those of the eastern Mediterranean in general. There was no comparison between these workers, more trim than their English counterparts would be, and the coarse, crude longshoremen of Piraeus or Limassol. As they worked, strange, beautiful, umbrella-shaped jellyfish, bluish with a dark band round them, perhaps a foot long, gathered round the ship, floating just under the surface of the brilliantly clear, blue-greenish water. Someone said they were called medusas. I was not sure whether the name was quite appropriate or not, but could not dispute it.

Facing us was Jaffa to the right, and Tel Aviv to the left, their combined waterfront of five miles or so being visible in great detail in the bright sunlight. The modern city, with its square concrete blocks of buildings, contrasted sharply with Jaffa, old-fashioned and studded with minarets. Although the two towns are now one, the division between East and West was quite clearly marked, seen from my ship; a thick, dark belt of trees, almost the only ones visible except for a few scattered ones in the Arab sector, was the approximate dividing line.

It may have been my first day in Israel, as far as territorial waters went, but it was not my first day on Israeli ground, so I decided not to count it as the first of my Israeli life. Technically speaking, as I was on an Italian ship, I was presumably still in Italy, anyway. I found it in no way annoying to be so near and yet so far. After all, it was the Israeli countryside I was fundamentally aiming at. Having lived in London nearly all my life, it did not matter if I never saw a town again; such a deprivation, if necessary, would be but a light one. And, of course, it would not be necessary in any case. There would be plenty of future years in which to see Tel Aviv–Jaffa from the inside, so what did today matter?

The evening ride along the Israeli coast, with groups of lights denoting towns and settlements, was surely the most romantic of my life. At the end of the fifty or so miles, the lights of Haifa appeared, littered generously all over Mount Carmel, itself rather indefinite under the half-moon. Just after eleven o'clock the ship anchored outside the harbor ready to enter early next morning.

November 1

We started to move into the harbor before seven; within half an hour we were duly tied up at the wharf. The Customs people then boarded again, but this time it was not felt necessary to greet them with any appreciable enthusiasm. Eventually they stamped my passport and passed me on to the Ministry of Health representative at the next table in the first-class salon. The latter never bothered to look at the official Medical Card and Vaccination Certificate about which so much fuss had been made in London. He merely asked me whether I had been vaccinated and, on my referring to the Certificate, passed me to the last table: Currency Control. How much money had I? Exactly none. No dollars? I laughed. That was that.

November 7

It has been such an involved week of all sorts of complicated official negotiations and arrangements that it was just impossible to record all the details; and, anyway, it does not matter, for such things are purely personal and passing. From the moment I actually landed on the quay at Haifa Port I certainly found everyone very helpful, and, while keeping within the bounds of inevitable officialdom, there was a reasonable flexibility everywhere.

To summarize it all very briefly, I wandered about considerably in my first five Israeli days, centering on Haifa itself, where I was temporarily housed by the Jewish Agency, and visiting a kibbutz which proved quite unsuitable for a lone Englishman. Afterwards I was directed, all expenses paid, to Kibbutz Hazorea, fifteen miles southeast of Haifa, where I was immediately accepted as a working guest, and thus passed out of the care of the Jewish Agency into that of the kibbutz itself. I shall describe this kibbutz in some detail in this diary. All I need record now is that on my arrival, towards the close of my fifth day in the country, I was given a sort of a cabin to live in, and then allowed a couple of work-free days to settle down and get used to the surroundings as well as possible.

November 8

It has now been agreed that I should be put on light work for a start and join the sheep department in a day or two. I spent my first day at work in Israel puttying glass into frames destined for use in the kitchen garden as protection for cucumbers or something like that. By the time I got up speed, after a few uncertain hours at the start, I estimated that I was manipulating the pseudo-plasticine into sausagelike lengths, pushing it into position and smoothing it off with an old knife, or, better, with my thumbs and fingers, at a rate of something like eight meters an hour. My supervisor seemed satisfied with the results. One or two boys helped me at the outset, but I was on my own nearly all day in a corner on the hillside. Apart from putting my hand through a pane of glass at the very beginning of operations—the glass being far less strong than I thought—all went well. Even the breakage was of no importance; my assistants quickly nailed a few old replacement sections into place. The frames constituted an extraordinary patchwork quilt of old pieces of glass. I managed not to cut myself too much. As a glazier, I might have a future, but I fear this occupation might pall in the long run.

I took some readings with my thermometer from England at 1:20, in the hour-and-a-half lunch break. Seventy-three degrees in the shade, and 95° in the sun. Nothing ex-

treme: possibly a little less than during my first week in
the country, but still brilliant hot summer weather from
the English point of view—and this first day of my second
Israeli week, on which I began work for my new country,
was also the first day of the second week of November!

November 9

Worked a while in and near the silo, which has grain-
cleaning and other machines in the bottom. This tall
square structure of brick and concrete is the dominant one
in the place—an infrequent feature, since the water tower
is usually the most prominent. Our water tower, however,
is half hidden in trees on the hillside and is not very tall
anyway. The balcony of the "flat" occupied by a family
on its top, as I later discovered, nevertheless afforded a fine
view all over the *meshek*, or farm establishment, as one
might say.

For the main part of the morning I became a "garbage
man." I was particularly pleased about this, although it
was, of course, a messy job: I helped collect garbage cans
and convey them by tractor and trailer to the rubbish
dump where their contents were burned. Still, from the
equalitarian standpoint, it is right that everyone should be
a garbage man occasionally, rather than let a few under-
dogs form a depressed class by being garbage men all the
time. Before my initiation into the profession of garbage-
manship I was told to fill in an interval with a feeble attempt at road making, but this was not very successful. The
implement employed for spreading the powdered rubble
was a spade with its blade at right angles to the shaft (I am
told this type of tool is not allowed in England, but I have
no idea why; I have certainly never seen it there, though),

and one has to hold it at a much lower angle than an ordinary spade or the stuff falls off too soon.

In the afternoon, I had to sort out numerous sacks into three piles—good, bad, and indifferent (worth repairing). This work was done in a shed in which enough grain was lying about loose to form a highly extravagant and superfluous carpet. The final item in the operations in this shed happened to be the same as my very first job after I left school seventeen-and-a-half years ago: untying string. There were over four hundred pieces of sack strings to untie and tie into handy bundles of fifty.

November 10

Detailed to the sheep at last. I called at the little office of the work manager, below the doorway steps of the dining hall, for instructions the evening before, in accordance with the regular procedure (I am No. 106 on the huge, ruled work sheets for the men, but there are probably as many women and there are various outside groups as well), and was made assistant shepherd. It was also my first rainy day in Israel. Yesterday it had been quite cloudy, for the first time in my brief experience here, and I had wondered whether some of the clouds, which certainly suggested rain, heralded the approach of the wet winter season, which people said would start any time now. My guess was right for I was awakened at 1:20 A.M., by loud peals of thunder, lightning, and rain which continued intermittently and diminishingly until nearly midday, by which time the whole meshek was quite a quagmire. It appears that, when the time does come, the rainy season starts here with a bang. The 330 sheep, however, showed no interest one way or the other. They were otherwise engaged, and I spent most of the day in separating the ewes due to lamb in December from the remainder due to lamb later, so as to give the first group extra rations from now on.

The procedure included a remarkable amount of passing the sheep in groups through doors and gates in and out of their large shed and the divided sections of their yard in front. The head shepherd caught the sheep, one by one, called out the number in Hebrew, stamped on a metal tag affixed in one ear, and held the animal while the assistant shepherd looked up its number in a tabulated list in a rather dirty exercise book. If the ewe was listed as due to lamb in December, the second shepherd would call out to me (also in Hebrew; I soon understood the words without interpretation by the head shepherd), and I, standing by with paint pot and brush, would blodge its neck with a good splosh of red.

November 11

Even apart from those engaged on special services who, naturally, have to vary their rest days, not everyone has his weekly rest day on Sabbath. One can change it voluntarily, if one prefers some other day off; or the work manager may request one to alter it to fit in with a more suitable work schedule from the point of view of the group. Anyway, I had my weekly rest day after only three days' work. On the same day I had to vacate my first room, which had to be put at the disposal of a brilliant young producer-theater-critic-cum-kitchen-worker from Ireland, who returned for a weekend amateur dramatic show from a seminar he was giving to another kibbutz. I had to transfer my things to a smaller hut which was much more picturesque because it was completely swathed in creeper.

The procedure was interrupted very pleasantly by my

first Anglo-German friend who, in a before-lunch walk, took me on a conducted tour of the meshek and explained the geographical setting when seen from the heights. I had known virtually nothing of the detail before, apart from the dining hall, the sheep shed opposite one end of it, and the cowsheds nearer my hut. I was therefore extremely gratified to be shown the children's houses (one for each main age group), splendidly designed and outfitted, the new medical block in the process of being built (with doctor's room, dentist's room, dispensary, patients' waiting room, etc.), and the parents' bungalow blocks. My friend also showed me with pride the carpentry workshop in which he himself worked. It was one of the largest in Israel, although not comparable with a factory, piled with fine examples of school, hospital, and other furniture, which goes all over the country.

The homemade operetta in the evening, staged to commemorate an anniversary of the orchards, was a highly amusing parody of the doings of the orchard department in terms of ancient Greece, complete with Hercules, Atlas, Zeus, and so on. I could not, of course, understand the Hebrew, but the music, by our local composer-member, struck me as being quite pleasing in a truly modern, lightweight, but beautifully finished style. The tunes, sometimes nondescript, but often of an oddly abrupt structure with a delightful twist in the tail, could be compared with the sort of thing Benjamin Britten has done, admittedly much more grandly, in *Let's Make an Opera,* and, for a kibbutz composition, I think that is praise enough. It is impossible to say less, though: the best tune was still being sung around the place a fortnight later, as a matter of fact, and, in the end, I got to know it quite thoroughly myself.

After the performance (which was repeated twice the

next day, for the children at teatime and for the rest of the adults in the evening) we had very nice biscuits—the first I had seen in Israel, they being obviously rarities kept for special occasions—and green, but inside quite ripe, mandarin oranges passed round the crowded benches in the dining hall. Then the benches were put aside, the planks disposed of through the windows and the floor cleared for dancing to music from the piano. I watched the dancing for quite a time: it was, as in ancient days, an expression of human joy in a variety of patterns with all sorts of Balkan and other folk ingredients included, to say nothing of excellent old-fashioned waltzes gaily whirled.

November 13

Gathering nuts in May has given way to a new occupation—gathering cauliflower leaves in November. In a field across the road, heads of cauliflower are cut for market and I, with the intermittent aid of whichever one of the three main shepherds is on duty with me, pick the leaves afterwards for the sheep. The crop, after several hours' work, comes to about half a ton, packed in nearly thirty sacks which are collected by horse and cart when ready and brought to the sheepshed for distribution in the feeding troughs. This is the sheep's dinner. For tea, they have corn straw, and for breakfast grain which comes in sacks weighing about forty kilos (or about eighty-eight pounds) and which are decidedly difficult to carry about and empty into the troughs. These are followed later by bundles of hay which are only half as heavy and therefore much easier to handle. The sheep have no evening meal at all, but, if they want to, they can make their straw last all night by eating it slowly.

In the evening, another excellent young German who

knew English very well came to my room to arrange Hebrew lessons. He, unfortunate fellow, had been detailed to teach me. We fixed approximately two evenings a week. While doing so, we were interrupted by the sound of machine gunning and of heavier guns going off in the hills. "It might be serious," my teacher-to-be commented. We went outside. Several people were standing about looking at the flashes to the west. Short of the Egyptian navy landing at Atlit, I could not imagine how any Arab attack could possibly come from that side. "Only exercises," we heard in a minute or two. But it appeared that such sounds had not been heard for two years previously. Assuming that the sounds reach as far as Jordan, it seems quite a good idea to make a noise occasionally, just to keep the Arabs quiet.

November 14

I was faced with an awkward problem this morning, for no one turned up at 6 A.M. to help me with the sheep's breakfast. There was little hope of finding anyone who knew English and who could correct the position. Actually I did speak to one or two people later, but although they understood, they could not help. I decided to clean out the troughs with a hand brush, as usual, and then carry on with the grain and the seeds we sprinkle on top of it. There were plenty of seeds, but only two sacks of grain instead of the four required. After two hours instead of the usual one or so, I let the sheep in from the yards to a strictly rationed breakfast. Meanwhile they had become extremely wet in a thunderstorm, but apparently rain does not hurt them. Their wool is very greasy naturally. Incidentally, they are not grown for their wool, but primarily for their milk, which is turned into cheese. Their second value is in their meat; the wool is so coarse that it comes a poor third, useful only for rugs and carpets, although in times of great austerity it can be used for coarse clothing as well.

While I was having my own breakfast, the head shepherd came up to me. He had just returned from a political mission in Haifa: a politically conscious kibbutz like ours does its best in such directions. I explained matters. It turned out there had been a most unusual confusion with work schedules and days of rest and a misunderstanding had ensued with the second (or was it the third?) shepherd. Anyway, the head shepherd approved my action and explained that there was plenty more grain in sacks at the opposite end of the shed.

Hazorea already boasts a private railway. The main line down the Emek does not work now and has a doubtful future; it never paid its way, even under British control before the War of Independence, so much more important has road transport always been in modern Israel. The Hazorea branch is about fifty meters (or fifty-five yards) long and quite devoid of mechanical tractive power. The route is meant to be straight, but has a most unfortunate kink in the middle which makes derailment almost inevitable. It connects the milk-cooling section of the cow department with the sheepshed, so that the sheep's milk can also be cooled. The cowshed end also serves the kitchen, at the back of the dining hall, and enables kitchen waste to be brought to the sheep at the cost of probably more labor and time than would be consumed in carrying it directly, except in the case of really heavy loads, which, however, are rarely available. The rolling stock is a trolley, which must be pushed by hand: and the less said about the rails, the better. Occasionally it is necessary to unearth these somewhat, as they are inclined to disappear altogether in places, while other stretches rest entirely on the surface, being neither embedded nor anchored. There is a bridge, too, on the route: that is to say the line runs, unsupported, across a rainwater drainage canal. The chief use of the line at present is for children who love to give each other rides on the trolley.

I have already discovered that the most frequently used word in the Hebrew language is *"Ma?"*—"What?"—and it is evidently not considered at all rude to keep on saying it, as it would be in English. (Nor, for that matter, is it considered rude to put one's elbows on the table, which is, after all, often the best place for them. Manners are, in fact, considerably more practical than in Britain, although the amount of true courtesy is probably greater.) Oddly enough, *"Ma?"* is also the persistent interrogation of the sheep. They have, no doubt, become completely Hebraized since their Arabic-speaking days, when their former native masters never raised them to anything like modern standards. Incidentally, with their mostly brown faces and long, shaggy, thick, coarse wool, they look to me more like imaginary baby yaks than anything like the Southdown sheep I used to know so well. Their tripartite, foot-wide trails, of which only the middle section, when discernible, bears any resemblance to a customary tail, is another odd feature to English eyes. At present, the two sections of the flock mostly ignore each other; but when conversation does ensue between the December-lambing ones and the others across the yard fence, one can easily imagine its trend, between innumerable *Ma*'s thrown back and forth.

Just to close these miscellaneous notes before returning to the journal proper, a final footnote about clothes. The feature which pleases me most is that one never wears a jacket, but only a pullover, if necessary. The sense of phys-

ical freedom gained is quite marvelous. Some people do
have American-type jackets, and I, too, may have one
some day, but I am in no hurry. And as to the idea of wearing a tie in Israel—it is merely comical to me, although
one does see such sights in Haifa.

November 22

I had a wonderful skirmish in the sheepshed today. The
job was to repaint the red sheep, i.e., the ones which had a
blob of red on them already, since the previous blobs had
worn off. The sheep were not at all keen on the idea, reason unknown, as it could not possibly hurt them. They
jumped about like mad when I aimed my brush at their
necks, with the result that many of them got daubed on
their tails, and much of the paint went over me instead of
them. But it was great fun—for me, even if the sheep did
not enjoy it as much as they should have.

November 25

I had another Shabbat walk today, which started as a
very small affair up what we call "our hill." This is the
one which runs right down to the farmyard, and in fact,
my hut is on the last inch or two of it. We wanted to get
as close a view of the sea as we could. It was rather disap-
pointing, being but a narrow strip somewhere north of
Haifa Bay towards the Lebanon frontier; but the general
views across the Emek were grand. I continued along the
top in the hope of reaching Mishmar Haemek, but distances seem infinitely longer on top of the hills than along
the road, and when I eventually crossed the ruins of an
Arab village and dropped down to the road, with considerable difficulty owing to very rough ground, I found that
I was not far past Hazorea. At any rate, I walked back in

ten minutes. On the way I saw the fruit of prickly-pear cactus plants for the first time and brought back a specimen from the ruins—a highly prickly fruit, pinkish, soft, tubular, and the size of a lemon. Afterwards I heard one could eat these fruits, after skinning them cautiously. But I let mine get too squashy to experiment: I must try again later.

November 26

For the first time, one of the shepherds took me along to the hills with the sheep for half a day. Previously, I had gone only to local roadside pastures a few minutes' walk from the farmyard itself. They had begun to leave me alone with the sheep in these places. There had been no difficulty except that the peppers and other valued plants at the edge of the pasture had to be guarded to avoid their being eaten. But now we went two or three kilometers up the main track to the hills, alongside the wadi, with the half-flock trailing along behind; the other shepherd on hill duty took the other half-flock separately. I came back for the midday dinner; the sheep, however, stayed with the shepherd—it was not worthwhile bringing the slow-moving animals an hour's walk to and fro—for that is roughly the time they take to get to their grazing grounds. The other shepherd had a sandwich with him, of course.

A good deal of control is needed to get the sheep past the "forest" without letting them nibble at the new trees. This is nearly as tricky as preventing the sheep from getting run over by the traffic on the main road. The basic life aim of any healthy sheep (and the Hazorea ewes all seem to be extremely healthy) seems in general to be in the wrong place at the wrong time and do the wrong thing. If they cannot manage to block three or four trucks on the road with much attendant confusion, they make up for it by invading the forest as hungrily as possible instead of keeping to the path. Anyway, as a result of this I saw much more of the hills and the forests than I had on my previous day's walk. Woods would probably be a better word than forests, since the tree areas are quite small: a few dozen acres on a hillside makes a typical block of afforestation; but as the blocks get linked up and more hillsides are planted, a junior forest will eventually result.

November 29

The first job today was mushrooming! Curiously, I had never succeeded in managing any in England, but here it was quite easy—the forest is fairly well populated, with the yellowish mushrooms said to have been originally and accidentally imported with the fir trees from France. They have turned out to be a very valuable autumnal crop; people are drafted from any and every department to go off by truck and fill as many tins as possible, emptying them into large, flat wooden boxes. Most of the work consists of carrying the tins up and down the extremely steep hillsides. I understand the mushrooms are sold at a high price in the cities.

Opposite the door of my hut, at one end of the great barn, a cow was installed, complete with lamp. The segregated animal, suitably tied up, must have been ill. Too ill to read, I suppose, as the lamp was taken away some time later.

December 1

The second film show since I arrived at Hazorea took place tonight in the dining hall after supper. The pictures, projected on a large white sheet with Hebrew captions shown concurrently down one side, was very effective. It was an Eskimo film, *Mala the Magnificent,* and was preceded by a short about Dr. Jenner of vaccination fame. A fortnight before—the programs are approximately fortnightly, the films and apparatus touring the kibbutzim accordingly—a very boring French cartoon had preceded two Russian films. Of these, the first was superbly effective from my point of view, showing Russian dances with their appropriate music from many parts of the Soviet Union. The other, a long film about Russian life in the last few decades, was incomprehensible to me since I could understand neither the Russian dialogue nor the Hebrew captions provided.

December 2

Shabbat—but more mushrooms required while the short season lasts, so there was half a day's work after all. It was the first gray day since I had arrived in Israel: cloudy all the time after a bright morning, veiled only by early mist. At 7:30 A.M. the temperature was actually as low as 47° F.

The children's orchestra was rehearsing in the afternoon, as I found out when I inspected the source of the sounds coming from the dining room. It seemed to be mainly an orchestra of recorders, but a few other instruments made valiant attempts to reduce the general squeakiness of tone. It was really very charming to see the little ones making music in concert so seriously under the guidance of their teacher, a senior worker.

December 3

I had a slight shock when I was told this morning that I was to take the sheep out to the hills by myself for the first time. It seemed rather odd to be given sole charge of one or two hundred valuable sheep (later I found they were worth at least twelve Israeli pounds each, so that when one takes a flock out for a walk one roams about with one or two thousand pounds' worth of sheep) after I had accompanied the experienced shepherds only about half a dozen times and only over part of their terrain. But there it was. Actually, I found that nothing very serious could go wrong. The worst that could normally happen was that the sheep would stand still and do nothing, instead of proceeding along smoothly. On the whole, we got on quite well together. I had learned to make the long trilled *"r"* noise at them, which serves as the standard call. After learning Spanish, an almost indefinitely prolonged trill is simple; what was more difficult was to get a rising and falling tone into it, but I managed that too in the end, although I doubt whether it sounded really professional. I ignored consistently the other weird cries ejaculated at the poor animals by the shepherds. I do not think they are at all essential, and I am all for the utmost simplicity of approach once friendly contact has been established. My greatest difficulty lay in the fact that I was not at all sure of the limits of the Hazorea grazing grounds, but I played for safety by going only where I had been taken before, and things worked out quite all right in the end.

There was a Hanukka party for the children in the dining room at teatime. It was a semiceremonial occasion: the room was crowded with admiring parents while some of the children lit the candles and recited whatever they had learned for the occasion. With the songs and the decorated surroundings, another little bit of modern Israel came true for me.

December 5

For a change, a new job today: tree planting. It was particularly interesting to take part in this vital work of improving the face of the land. Rather like mushroom picking, most of the work consisted of walking up and down the extremely steep hillsides. One of the most interesting aspects of the affair was that I was working with Yemenites. Young or old, they were nearly all very friendly people, some with the traditional side curls. They dug the holes in which the saplings were to go—quite large holes for the relatively tiny treelets, but a cleared space around no doubt gives the young tree a better chance. Little pine trees they nearly all were, with a few cypresses for the bottom of the hill to make the boundary of the forest next to the dirt track along which I normally take the sheep. The kibbutz member superintending operations (the Yemenites were outside workers from a neighboring village of their own) was certainly one of the Germans, so I mentally named him *der Waldmeister,* after the Johann Strauss operetta, the overture to which I have on a record. Both he and his assistant originally agreed that the little four-inch trees should be pressed into the soil extremely firmly. But when the man who afterwards turned out to be the very august Chief Inspector of Forests for Northern Israel, with his base at the kibbutz up the other end of the dirt track some half a dozen kilometers away, arrived in his jeep to do some inspecting, he ordered that relatively gentle pressure should be applied. An enormous argument in vigorous Hebrew developed, but inevitably the Chief Inspector won, so I had to change my working methods accordingly.

It was the turn of the grown-ups to have their Hanukka party today, but except for many decorations it was not particularly exciting.

December 6

A new job for the sheep today. It consisted of going to the main storehouse, helping to haul bags of varieties of bran and similar substances into a central position, tipping them out to make a giant heap weighing about a ton, and, with another person opposite one, turning the whole heap over onto a fresh position, using spades, and then turning it back again, to make sure it was properly mixed. It was. A little salt was sprinkled on the mountain of sunflower seed, bonemeal, and whatnot, and sacks of crushed carobs were emptied in, too. These dried, broken carob beans, occasionally obtainable cheaply in more or less complete condition in England, are quite nice to eat, being sweet, and the sheep and I equally approve of them. I did not get on so well with the other constituents of their nourishing concentrate, though. When we had composed it in bulk, the shield-shaped spades with the long handles had to be brought into use again to rebag it in about thirty sacks which were conveniently stretched over a double metal tripod affair for holding them open while being filled. The last process of all was to tie up the full sacks for subsequent transport to the sheep shed. One way and another, this was quite a job: I hope the sheep will be duly grateful.

December 7

After taking something like two hundred twenty sheep to pasture in the morning, I finished up by attending a milking demonstration in the evening, which is to say that I looked on, as well as I could, while the head shepherd milked some of the few sheep which had already lambed. In a way, there seemed to be nothing to milking, but it remains an interesting mystery I shall have to find out about in practice later on.

December 8

This evening, the first phonograph concert took place since my arrival at Hazorea. It comprised, of all things, part of the Glyndebourne recording of *Così fan tutte;* of all things, because I was a Mozart lover and had lived within walking distance of Glyndebourne in Sussex. Reproduction in the dining room through record player and powerful radio was excellent. I was struck by the beautiful effects, understanding now much better than previously what Mozart was driving at in this subtle work. But a tiny audience of about thirty had dwindled to half that number by the end. I could not imagine what they were thinking about. Too bad, especially considering there were so many Germans here who certainly have had the right background. I hope we shall do better than this in the near future.

December 9

More mushroom picking in the morning, in a different part of the forest. It was not exactly compulsory this time, but I like picking things anyway, so a short session of an hour or two suited me all right.

With the fading of the daylight, I at last walked south along the main road to our neighboring kibbutz, the famous Mishmar Haemek, and back. It took me just about forty minutes each way, walking quite fast, as the temperature has dropped considerably lately, since the beginning of the rainy season. Now, in early December, it was something like an English spring or autumn. I spent a quarter of an hour walking around Mishmar Haemek, impressed by its beautiful avenues of palm trees. I could not understand what the large, long, and high concrete factory at one end of the place was for; after I returned I learned that it was the noted regional secondary school to which children over twelve years old go daily from Hazorea and other kibbutzim of the district. For children of more distant kibbutzim, the establishment was also run as a boarding school. Yet Mishmar Haemek, in spite of its extensive residential area of many and varied concrete buildings, did not strike me as particularly attractive. I did not venture into the actual farmyard section, where I would necessarily have looked too obviously an interloper. Had I been asked to explain my presence there, I could not have done it adequately in Hebrew, and it was doubtful whether the predominantly Polish population would know much English. Of course, the magnificent dining hall looked very fine, but, in general, the place seemed vague, untidy, and sprawling: haphazard, in a word. From subsequent information acquired back home, I gathered that the degree of planning at Mishmar Haemek was never as great as that at Hazorea; the place did, in fact, grow bit by bit, much as London did. But it would be absurd to judge it yet, for, although twice as old as Hazorea, it had suffered very serious damage in the War of Independence and was now in a state of new growth as well as repair.

December 12

Today the dining room looked like an art gallery, the walls covered with reproductions of paintings of all varieties ranging from modern Central European fantasies to classics and Degas and Cézanne. The members were told to write their choices (each picture was numbered) on a list and after drawing the numbers from a hat, the pictures would be distributed among them to decorate their rooms for a period until another change-round took place. I have heard vaguely of some such scheme having been mooted and perhaps actually working in England; as to Hazorea, it gets on with this popular art appreciation quite as a matter of course. There is no doubt about our being civilized here! It seems the art teacher at the Mishmar Haemek secondary school, who lives here, is responsible, having assembled a large collection of these reproductions, of which fifty were on show.

December 16

On the way home with the sheep, I heard cries coming from the place where one crosses the tiny river running down the wadi to take a short cut into the meshek. When I reached the spot with my flock, I found that one of the sheep from the other shepherd's flock had managed to get stuck in a patch of mud alongside the water. I tried to pull it out but failed, so reported it on return. The other shepherd quickly effected the rescue. He said it was quite an easy thing—if you know how, that is. Apparently, the method is to haul the front legs out first and then push from behind so that the whole animal arrives on dry land. Sheep are so clumsy at times. . . . Incidentally, I never noticed a single cloud in the sky all day, but I did notice a delightful smell from our fig trees—or are they something else?—in bloom.

December 17

I had the day off to go to Haifa by bus to see about my luggage, which had been reported as having arrived at the port. I obtained the release from the shipping agents all right, and even got on quite well at the port, after wasting most of the morning in queues, but just as things began to look promising I was told nothing further could be done without my passport and the booklet the Jewish Agency had given me on arrival. As I happened to have left my passport with my cousin, who had it at home up Mount Carmel, and the booklet was in the office at Hazorea, that was the end of proceedings for the day. When I caught the bus back, it was one of our own drivers who was in charge. On driving through our gate, he was greeted by his child who climbed aboard to be driven up our farm road to the bus turning point a hundred yards or so ahead.

December 19

The impossible happened today—the flocks became mixed! As I was coming home down the last stretch by the wadi, I saw the other shepherd passing along the main road with his flock in front of me at right angles. I naturally pulled up short, so as to give him time to continue along his different route. But my sheep had seen their friends ahead and were not at all willing to stay separated. For all that, by rushing around madly in front, I managed to check them—for a minute. Then some of them became rather too clever. They started infiltrating sideways into a field of olive trees which was a short cut home. I do not say this was a planned diversion, of course, but it had the effect of one, for while I was chasing them back out of the field, the others moved forward along the proper route and, before I could again get ahead of them, were out on the main road running after the other flock which was still far from out of the way. A terrific skirmish followed on the road, but there was much too much width to guard, including the border of weeds and the ditch, across which many of them scrambled. In view of the danger that some of the sheep would get run over by the truck traffic passing, it became hopeless to continue the battle, and the flocks duly won by mixing themselves up thoroughly. We hardly bothered to try to unmix them after getting them into their home yards in front of the shed; by that time it was getting too dusky to see their red blobs.

December 20

As it happened, I was put in another department of work today: the general farmyard branch, which is engaged in internal transport, grain handling at the elevator mill, hay and straw dumping, and so on. Today's work consisted mostly of riding around on a trailer behind a tractor and piling up bits of wood and piles of weed destined for the rubbish dump. This had to be done before the extensive rains (which were expected) made the ground too muddy to get around. So I heard no more about the mixed-up sheep and, in the end, it appeared that the mingled flocks caused no appreciable trouble after all, because they were going to be re-sorted anyway: thus the disaster was quite minimal.

At midday, I saw our Haifa bus driver enjoying a brief lift on a trolley behind a tractor across the farmyard, as a change from his customary more glorious type of transport.

December 22

Yet another Haifa trip, following upon a further one yesterday. The complications with the authorities at the docks are quite incredible. The delays in getting the Customs to examine one's luggage defy description. After going back specially early this morning, the Customs officer took until nearly lunchtime to dispose of my seven cases, taking immense interest in my radio, record player, and records. In the end he was satisfied and, after much more running about from office to office to get papers filled in and stamped, he granted duty-free clearance. Dock charges will have to be paid later when a Hazorea truck fetches the goods. Having conveyed me yesterday, our bus driver brought me back again today. Compared with London bus experience, it seems odd to be able to sit at the same dinner table with one's bus driver! It would be particularly interesting if he knew much English, but I doubt if he does.

Returning an hour later than was anticipated, I spent the rest of the afternoon picking tomatoes with the second of two Egyptian newcomers, both called Moshe. It was quite confusing to distinguish them. But this Moshe speaks Spanish, whereas the other one, in spite of having a Sephardi father, does not. So I practiced some of my Spanish with him during the tomato picking.

Shabbat eve supper actually included a small, very ripe banana—my first in Israel.

December 23

I made a list of the Hebrew headings to the columns on the large daily worksheets which show the members' assignments. Established members have their names printed in permanent position; newcomers are penciled in at the bottom. Both the men's and women's sheets total about a hundred names each, and there are certain supplementary lists. The Hebrew titles of the various branches of the economy take a good deal of learning.

December 24

Today's work involved poisoning mice. A party of people go out to the fields on a trolley drawn by a tractor; they are armed with spoons and small tins, which are filled from a large can of pink grains of wheat or something similar. The brigade then marches slowly in line, a short distance apart, and drops about five of the poisoned grains by the side of any mousehole observed in the course of transit across the fields of wheat, barley, clover, or other crop. The finale is taken for granted: the mice are expected in due course to come out and commit suicide as required. As fields here are likely to measure half a kilometer by a quarter of a kilometer, the amount of walking necessary for adequate coverage is considerable, not that it is noticeable to a habitual walker, which I happen to be. Apart from the walking, the work is, of course, trivial. The holes usually occur in colonies, so a burst of "work" is followed by a quiet period of walking with one's eyes fixed to the ground. I was interested to find that the party included a Chilean girl, on loan to Hazorea from Kibbutz Sardi, visible as a cluster of very white buildings on the hillside immediately across the Emek. I was able to make my Spanish work quite all right with her, as it also did with the second of the two Egyptian Moshes, he again acting as a workmate.

Radishes have replaced tomatoes as standard subsidiary diet at almost all meals now. Apparently there are many hundredweights to use up. Red jam has returned to the teatable, but it is impossible to say whether it is any relation of strawberry jam; very unlikely, I should say.

December 25

Christmas Day—as our cheerful Irish theater-producer from London reminded me yesterday by wishing me a merry Christmas with a broad grin. A warm and wonderfully brilliant day: I do not think there was a cloud in the sky all day long, but there was a morning mist across the Emek, leaving the hills rising clear above on each side. Sometimes, when one is working far out in the Emek fields in the early morning, the mist is thick enough to cut one off entirely from the meshek. As one leaves the kibbutz behind half a kilometer back at the foot of the hills, and rides out behind a tractor to the workplace, the hills disappear and one can easily imagine one is working in the flat, far-stretching fields of an English county like Essex.

Today it was mouseholes in the morning and picking carrots in the afternoon, sitting on boxes to pull the tops off the carrots afterwards before putting them into boxes for subsequent transport. The truck-garden output must be enormous here: it feels odd to be a worker behind the scenes helping to supply the Haifa housewives.

December 31

I embarked upon my first session of sheep milking. It was far from successful. I did get some milk out of those unfortunate animals which fell into my hands in the milking room at one end of the sheepshed. The milking stands are arranged on a concrete platform on which the sheep stand with their heads secured by bars. By simply adjusting the bars, the sheep can easily be imprisoned and released. I never realized before I came here how the job was done: the sheep are enticed to take up their positions and put their heads through the bars, which thereupon are closed upon their necks. While being milked, the animals amuse themselves quietly by eating the prepared mix, a concentrate flavored with sweet carob beans of which they are so fond that they rush for it as soon as they are let into the milking room. In fact, the rush is so great that often two heads become stuck in the place for one, here and there, and murder is likely to ensue when the bars are closed in position, unless one notices it in time to avoid strangulation and forces the superfluous sheep to a vacant place.

Although I squeezed out small quantities, my milking really was deplorable. I could not develop a proper grip: my hands kept slipping off the teats, and even after taking ten minutes per sheep instead of two, I left half the milk behind. Obviously, much patient practice will be required.

January 2

A middle-aged *moshavnik* came to us today for six months' training with the sheep, the idea being that he would then go back to his *moshav,* or cooperative village, in the Galilee hills, and be able to organize and run the sheep affairs of the place for himself and his neighbors. The arrangements were made by the Jewish Agency. The head shepherd had told me of them a few days ago, but nothing happened for a time, until it turned out someone had indeed come but had turned round and gone back again when he heard it involved work! If his successor stays, it will result in my being released for general work around the farm to a much greater extent than at present. I fully agreed with the head shepherd that this would be all to the good, for, exceptionally lucky though I have been in being able to begin to specialize right from the start, it is obviously unwise to do so before getting a broad view and at least some experience of the work of the place as a whole. According to Zionist publicity tracts, one's first year is meant to be quite generalized: it almost looked at first as if I were to miss this, but I am really glad to think I shall now get six months' general experience in any case.

January 4

At long last I have traced the whereabouts of my luggage. It has been at Hazorea for about a week and no one informed me until a chance remark put me on the scent! Eventually, the final dock complications had been cleared up, the charges most kindly paid for me by the secretariat, and the seven biggish cases brought here on a truck. They had been dumped in an outlying shed, along with some other luggage, and no one seemed to think there was the slightest need for me to get hold of the consignment at any particular time at all! Yet life will be very different when the radio gets going, to mention only one item. Today, four of the cases were brought along from the store by a tractor and unpacking commenced in the evening. What a job! I was advised not to have all the cases brought to my hut at once, as they would never go inside and rain might damage them if left outside—good advice, undoubtedly. I had two unexpected helpers with the unpacking; our moshavnik, and a Czech who seems to have come to join the kibbutz. I had spent much of the day chopping out an immense crop of weeds from between the eucalyptus saplings which form a row in front of our roadside barbed-wire fence. Perhaps I should say "behind," not "in front,"

for the trees are well inside the fence, and not by the side
of the road; it depends which way you look at it, or rather,
at them.

January 5

A great event took place this evening: a concert was
given at Mishmar Haemek by the Histadrut String Orchestra. This great trade-union organization's chamber group
was small like the Boyd Neel Orchestra, but in that magnificent hall, which has splendid acoustics, it sounded really
effective. The impression it made on me was comparable
to that of a chamber-orchestra concert in Wigmore Hall I
had heard a few months ago in London. I was told by others afterwards that, technically speaking, the playing and
conducting were largely unsatisfactory, but being a nonex-
pert listener myself, I was not disturbed more than once
or twice by erratic performance. Certainly the flamboyant
German conductor made the waltz from Tchaikovsky's
Suite for Strings sound excessively jolly, whereas I always
regarded it as an extremely doleful piece ever since I had
first heard it many years back. But his liveliness cut the
boredom for me out of a Vivaldi concerto grosso, and I
thought he and his players did quite brilliant justice to a
Mozart divertimento. A splendid male singer took part in
the concert and aroused justifiable enthusiasm with his
popular operatic arias. Two special buses transported the
considerable Hazorea contingent up and down the road,
but once we were there we seemed lost in the huge crowd,
for other neighboring kibbutzim had also sent detach-
ments. The expenses were shared among the participating
managements: the whole thing was free to individual kibbutznik concertgoers, of course.

January 8

Back in the forest once again. This time, instead of doing the actual planting, I was one of those digging the holes for the plants. This is not very formidable work: that part of the job was covered beforehand by my old friends, the picturesque Yemenites. They are the ones who cut the big gashes in the hillside, making basins to collect the rain around the young trees. All I had to do was to make a suitable little excavation for the tree itself halfway along the front of the oblong basin, at right angles to its axis; but even this required a technique of its own with the pickaxe. However, I soon got used to it, not that I became very efficient at it. I was anything but outstanding in the earlier part of the day's work, which involved weeding on a bank between trees planted a few months earlier: the *turiah,* or right-angled spade, is handled quite differently by the experts from the way in which I manipulated it. It is extraordinary that operations which look very simple always seem to have unexpected complications when one starts to do them.

January 12

Considerable excitement seems to have been caused by the arrival of my collection of 291 phonograph records, of which luckily only two broke en route. As soon as they were unpacked, our leading local musician arranged a concert of them for tonight. Unfortunately, reproduction was not too good, but it was not too bad either. The thirty or so people who were attracted by the notice on the bulletin board in the dining room seemed to have quite a good time with Mozart's overture to *Don Giovanni* and *Flute and Harp Concerto,* the theme and variations from Tchaikovsky's *Suite No. 3* in G, Respighi's *Brazilian Impressions,* and waltzes from *Die Rosenkavalier.* It was impossible to use my own sound system because the amplifier had been broken in transit, and the record player, when connected, gave an electric shock upon being touched. I placed both instruments into the trustworthy hands of our electrician for diagnosis and repair. The gathering took place in one of those classrooms which had been used for the recent art exhibition. Now the room was in its quaint customary condition, plastered all over with the children's works of art—the children here seem to indulge in an enormous amount of self-expression with colored pencils, and the results, surprisingly, are sometimes more than trivial.

January 15

The last of my luggage arrived at my hut by tractor. I stow away the contents of all the other five somehow.
turned two of the boxes into bookcases and am hoping to
Incidentally, this is my thirty-fourth birthday, and, having worked on Saturday, I had the day off as my weekly rest day—two days late, quite a common arrangement. At least one of the permanent shepherds has his Shabbats on the proper day, and I am called upon frequently to substitute with the sheep, having had at first a long unbroken run of Saturdays off.

In the evening I was visited by one of the German women with a particularly excellent command of English —apparently she had lived in England for many years— and given my first pocket money since the traveling expenses I had been given previously for my bus trips to Haifa. I am not at all clear about the pocket-money arrangements; but I cannot really expect to receive any regularly until the dock charges on my luggage are paid back. It appears that the German woman has been made responsible for looking after me and seeing that I have everything necessary in my room and so on; she is arranging for a kerosene stove to be provided, for instance. She must have been appointed by the committee which looks after the interests of newcomers. This is all very much more than I expected: the arrangements are more considerate here than I should ever have thought.

January 17

At teatime I was introduced to the Argentinian kibbutznik who works in the cow department. That is to say, he is German, but spent fourteen years in Argentina. I had a most interesting conversation with him in Spanish, although my Spanish is far from being adequate. He told me that the average milk yield of the cows here was over 4,000 liters (or about 1,000 gallons) a year which, I believe, is quite good. The Syrian-Dutch cows are known as respectable milkers.

January 20

Very euphemistically, the head shepherd invited me to attend a meat-testing session at nine o'clock this evening; in fact, he very kindly called for me just beforehand, as I was not too sure of the location of the meeting room, which was described as a clubroom for some of the North Africans. Now that we have so many newcomers from Morocco, Algeria, and Tunisia, French seems to be emerging as the second language of Hazorea. It is unfortunate that my knowledge of French is less than rudimentary; it would be useful with my Egyptian friends too, although their English is quite good. Evidently, it is just as well for *kibbutzniks* to be versatile linguistically. Anyway, when I got there, I found that the meat testing consisted of eating some lambs! The feast, followed by fried potatoes and fruit salad, was really excellent; I think I have never tasted quite such perfect meat in England. Arab fashion, we held the bones in our fingers to nibble at them; they were certainly worth picking!

The conversation had all been in Hebrew, of course, but the head shepherd very delightfully translated for me some little bits to keep me in touch here and there. When the feast was over, and the select group of shepherds and associates had cleared up their little party, I went to the dining room where the Bulgarian youth group and their friends were just about concluding one of their folk-dance sessions. The music was supplied by radio broadcast as part of the general, country-wide celebrations of the New Year of the Trees, on which school children go out into the fields and the hills to plant trees so vital for the agricultural development of the land.

Perhaps nothing at Hazorea has impressed me so much as these folk dances: for the most part East European in origin, by now they have become almost native to Israel. To watch the dancers' joyous abandon, in spite of the dances' considerable complication, is a most exhilarating experience. Here one comes in touch with the fundamental fascination of gay rhythm beating close to the very heart of life itself. In spite of my admiration for Scottish and Irish dance music, I never knew before that folk dancing could really mean such spontaneous joy.

January 21

Off to Haifa once more, to see about my radio repair and the claim on the insurance company for the few pounds of damage suffered by the luggage in transit to my new address. Negotiations were successful, but only after waiting nearly all afternoon for the radio shop to open. To my surprise I found it kept an extended siesta-lunch hour from midday to 4 P.M., quite worthy of Spain. This was the shop to which the Hazorea electrician had consigned the wireless set on finding that the damage was too great for him to cope with.

January 22

In spite of the advent of our moshavnik trainee, so far I seem to have almost as much to do with the sheep as ever, and my dubious incursions into other departments of the farm work remain relatively limited. Presumably, with time the moshavnik will be fitted into regular schedules. Anyway, on the way home with my flock today I was met by some of the Moroccan children, who staged quite a little rodeo, one or two of them actually succeeding in riding the sheep for quite a way, much to the sheep's obvious disgust, before falling off.

Not all the recent divertissements have been caused by children, though. Often in the mornings, a goat and a donkey are tied, a little way apart, to the side fencing of the track, where it leads past the kibbutz vegetable garden opposite Yoqneam village. I can never quite make up my mind whether these animals belong to us or to Yoqneam. At any rate, sometimes the goat tries to butt the passing sheep, who are quite ready for a fight until I urge them on. Often the sheep display inordinate curiosity towards the donkey, whom they apparently regard as having quite the wrong shape for a self-respecting member of their own sisterhood. They walk up to the donkey, peer at its back, front and sides, and stand around in a little circle, evidently appraising it critically, until the rest of the flock moves on and the inquisitive ones are left behind. Because of the flock instinct, this is the one thing they are more nervous about than the most nervous human child imaginable. The donkey, for his part, seems quite flattered by the attentions paid him and quietly gazes back.

January 29

I walked over to Tivon, this being my day off. Tivon, a noted garden suburb of Haifa, is partly visible on the crest of the ridge facing Hazorea across the Emek northwards. One goes six kilometers up the main road towards Haifa and then turns off over a bridge across the little River Kishon on to various tracks behind the rather untidy-looking settlement of Kiryat Haroshet, hoping one is following the right direction. As a matter of fact, I did get on the ridge at something like the right point, but became rather mixed up in the adjoining suburb of Kiryat Amal. For all that, I reached my cousins' house in Tivon in much less than two hours and had a good time there.

Although Tivon is quite pleasant, I do not see why it should be particularly noteworthy. Blocked by projecting lumps of the ridge on which it stands, its views are by no means as complete and sweeping as Hazorea's. It is, moreover, dominated, almost pressed down, by Mount Carmel hulking so closely over it with its enormous mass. Hazorea, on the other hand, is at just the right distance, so that the Carmel appears magnificently massive but not overwhelming. Tivon's most open view is northward to Haifa Bay, and the famous industrial development there does get rather in the way of a peaceful sea view. Still, it is a pleasant little place, perched as it is healthily high, with its attractive shopping center of half a dozen shops along one side of a square. While the mothers go into the shops they can leave their children on the lawn in the middle. The bungalows and houses are mostly of English style, in accordance with the taste of the immigrants, although most of them seem to be German-speaking. I fail to see that it is more attractive than any new London suburb, even though orange trees with large fruit ripening on them adorn some of the gardens. The term "garden suburb" surely suggests a place with large stretches of public gardens and cultivated roadsides, but Tivon does not go as far as that. It is, of course, unfinished as yet, several roads running through it being no more than half-made. No doubt it will be a very agreeable residential section once it develops a settled, gracious air, as it surely will in the future.

On the way back, I wandered into the meshek of Kibbutz Givat Zeid. A very simple, undeveloped layout: the place is not yet very many years old. Afterwards, I managed to reach the main road just in time for the midafternoon bus down to Hazorea.

January 30

There was an exhibition of new books in the library tonight, held in the reading room. About a dozen new English political and other works and a great number of Hebrew books were on display. The visitors could make their requests and the books would be made available for them in rotation.

February 1

Meeting the electrician in the evening, he asked me whether I knew my radio had come back from repair. I did not. So he showed it to me, put in a corner of the trac-

tor repair shed, found me a suitable plug for connecting
it up and handed it over. It certainly seems to work all right
now, but, apart from the local broadcasts which come in
very strong from Tel Aviv, I cannot find my way about the
dial, which is only natural. It will take quite a while to get
used to the stations one can receive here, so different from
Western Europe.

An issue of coffee, sugar, and a bar of chocolate was
made to everyone today, for consumption in one's own
room, by the way. A very nice idea: I never knew it existed
before. I am now told it takes place monthly—if the supplies arrive.

February 8

I think this has been the clearest day, atmospherically
speaking, since I have been here. The Galilean mountains,
probably thirty miles away, seem hardly more than a short
walk across the Emek, and the local hills on the eastern side
opposite might be virtually adjacent! One could clearly
see the mountains of Jordan, far in the south—although
usually these mountains are little more than a blue blur
in the distance. The atmosphere is, on the whole, much
clearer here than in England, but the winters evidently
contain many partly misty days so that the outlines are not
always sharp by any means, and a day like this is really exceptional, at this time of the year at any rate.

I happened to spend half my working day in the chicken
department (the *lul*) for the first time, but this did not
mean I had anything to do with the chickens themselves.
It merely involved helping to clean out one of their coops!
Afterwards, just for a change, I suppose, I was transferred
to hoeing an outlying field of beets—special, large-size
beets for cattle fodder, I was told—but the difficulty at this

early stage is to distinguish the beet from the diminutive weeds which have to be eradicated before they grow up to smother the wanted plants.

February 9

The second phonograph concert of my records took place tonight, but it was hardly successful, owing to the vagaries of the reproducing apparatus. The attractive program was advertised on the notice board, but only a dozen people, at the most, came to hear a Handel organ concerto, a Mozart horn concerto, Britten's *Young Person's Guide to the Orchestra,* Mossolov's *Steel Foundry,* and the *Waldmeister Overture* of Johann Strauss.

The record player insisted on revolving at a ludicrously slow speed, so that the organ effects at the outset were entirely absurd, and most of the audience gave up after a quarter of an hour of experimenting, and left. As it turned out, they were unwise, for soon thereafter all went well. In fact, I have never before heard my records perform so splendidly, for the radio used for amplification was double the size of my own. A small group of us had a magnificent evening.

February 15

In spite of the presence of the moshavnik, I continue to be nearly always with the sheep on their hill pastures. In fact, I have one flock and the moshavnik has the other, and sometimes we nearly meet. We both take care to prevent an actual meeting for fear of mixing the milking flock with the other one. The moshavnik, having no watch, calls across from the hill he may happen to be on to ask me the time, and I call back. As this does not always work when the wind is unfavorable, I sometimes have to raise my stick in the air the required number of times in order to signify the approximate hour.

Today, however, was one of the days when I was put on other work, and the transfer was most unusual: it was to the cowshed. It was not for any sort of regular work there, though: it was simply to carry the milk from each cow from one shed to the other where an official milk tester first weighed it and then tested it for butterfat content. The important point was to announce the name of each cow to the inspector, so that he could note her particulars for comparison with previous statistics—and very queer Hebrew names most of these animals have. Only a few sound very English indeed, even if spelled in Hebrew: Blackie, Lily, and so on. The latter were members of an American shipment, I heard. The machine-milker, a German whose English was near perfect, wrote the names on slips of paper for me to hold in my hand with the milk containers. This process took place at each of the three milkings during the day, but I was not required for the early morning session, only at midday and in the evening.

To my astonishment, I find the Hazorea railway has been repaired, and now nearly reaches the sheep shed. The sheep are producing so much milk now that it has actually been judged worth the time and trouble to improve the transportation from their shed to the dairy, where the churns are stored in refrigerated water tanks until they go to market at Haifa. My own milking is improving slightly, as I nearly always do a stretch of it after returning from the pasture. Theoretically this should take about an hour, but actually it comes closer to two. Time computation of a day's work with the sheep is very difficult, because one never knows what allowance, if any, to make for a lunch hour. If the sheep behave, one can sit down peacefully for quite a long time while they graze around; but if they are in a wandering mood one may have to eat lunch while on the move. No advance estimation is possible, for the sheep are hardly ever in the same mood two days running. I suspect they are sensitive to the slightest changes in the weather, even to small shifts in the wind, or, perhaps, to pressure and certainly to temperature changes.

February 19

After a walk of over three hours on my day off, I returned to find I had the chance of registering my desired change of name at the office on the special form concerned. Several such forms had recently been completed here, name changing being popular among the new immigrants as part of the process of acclimatization. I understand that the procedure does not become final legally for some months, but I have at any rate now applied for the new name of Avraham Haim Ben-Yosef in place of my original William Abraham Hyman Welsman.

February 20

I hear the Americans have arrived. Details are vague as yet but about thirty are supposed to be coming here for a six-month seminar, partly working, partly learning, so that they can go back and recruit others.

My radio yielded a magnificently impressive performance of Sibelius' *Fifth Symphony* early this evening by short wave from the B.B.C. I doubt if I have ever heard such a splendidly dramatic rendering. I heard this work only three or four times before in England, and this was the first time I was able really to understand what Sibelius was trying to do in this magnificent symphony. It now strikes me as being of quite the same order, if by no means quite the same, as Beethoven's symphonies. This is merely a personal impression, naturally, and maybe a passing one at that: a fleeting experience, anyway. But I think it is significant as showing the effective continuation of my music-loving life in new, very different surroundings.

My repeated visits to Haifa Port to get my luggage—I reckoned, in the end, that all in all I spent no less than thirteen hours there—are now bearing fruit. Surrounded by my hundreds of books and many more hundreds of booklets and papers—all appropriately sorted out and piled into an amazingly small space—I can now feel quite at home. Everything is at hand: in fact, everything is so much at hand that I can reach most of it without getting up from the little stool provided in the room to serve as a seat while I do my typing at my desk. All this, it is true, is not at all typical of kibbutz life in itself; it is merely my personal way of achieving a certain continuity, always, of course, subject to modifications as time goes on and I get settled in the new ways. I imagine, for instance, that much of my library will be incorporated into the kibbutz library in the years to come, if I succeed in becoming a full member here. Then its usefulness will be extended beyond me to others, but I shall be included among the "others" and shall rejoice all the more at what "my" books will come to mean to everybody. Special personal items can always remain in my hands in any case.

February 23

While on the hills with the sheep, I picked up two turtles for the second day running. I had never been so astonished, I think, as I was when I found my first turtle running about in the grass—well, not exactly running, but moving after a fashion. After all, in England, these animals

—or should I say reptiles?—are so artificial. One just buys them, or one did, in the long long ago, before the war. To see them crawling about in this country, free of charge, is really extraordinary in comparison. I again put my catches in the rough rucksack I carry on my back supplementary to the one I use for food and water; the real purpose of this rough knapsack is to bring back any lambs born en route, as newborn lambs cannot walk far at best, and one has to carry them home. Like such lambs, the tortoises were all too fond of climbing up and falling out; but, also like lambs, they are relatively bounceable and come to no harm. I usually wind up carrying the new lamb in my arms, the silly little quaint creature, but a turtle is a hopeless shape for that and it is too big to carry easily in one's hand. On each of the two days, one turtle was quite biggish and the other small, like a typical English pet. I try to keep them in boxes or baskets at my hut, but they do not seem to eat the leaves I provide—probably they are insect-eaters; I am not sure and nobody else seems to know either— but they clamber up and wander about almost hopelessly. I had placed the first two under a large, overturned box, one of the seven which had contained my luggage and which had been left outside my hut. In the box there were plenty of air holes, and grass and even insects were available. Today, however, when I got home I found that somebody had at long last removed the box, thereby allowing the turtles to escape, so that instead of a total turtle zoo of four, I was left with merely the two I brought home with me this time—and no adequate box to keep them in or under.

February 25

As a change from turtles (the remaining two have also escaped by now!), I picked up a splendid little toad outside the sheepshed. About four inches in size, it was beautifully marked with dark green blotches on greenish-gray, and its slippery, leathery skin felt delightfully cool in my hand. I let it go after a minute or two: toads are even more difficult than turtles to look after, considering the way they jump like mad!

February 26

For my Shabbat walk, I set off across the flat Emek, past our fields to the famous cooperative village of Nahalal. It took me three-quarters of an hour to follow the beaten-earth track to Kfar Yehoshua, the big cooperative village which one comes to first and which we see so well from Hazorea. It has large farm stores and equipment, operated collectively, and the big building in the middle seems to be a sort of town hall–community center. After some hesitation I decided that the only track available must be the one leading to Nahalal, which it turned out to be.

Nahalal was not very exciting when I got there. Its circular layout is acknowledged to look best from the air; on the ground it looks a typically vague and unfinished, if not untidy, modern village of small holdings. I do not want to insult current Israeli villages; they really are unfinished, perhaps almost without exception, since continual fresh immigration makes its mark on virtually every corner of the land and people are squeezed into every conceivable and inconceivable nook. But a person used to the long-settled, harmonious, old English villages is struck by their unnecessary untidiness, the bits of building material lying about everywhere, the haphazard gardens and paths, and the heaps of rubbish in incongruous places. I suppose a people frantically building up a new land simply do not have enough time to go in for artistic detail, even after several years, until they really get established. But I am bound to suspect that, on the whole, they do not really care about these things or they would find a way to look after them a little better. It seems that to have a neat little square concrete bungalow is as far as the ordinary East European imagination goes at present, and people cannot be bothered as yet about straight-edged footpaths and neat gardens. It would be ridiculous to criticize these people harshly. There are plenty of years ahead. They will get everything straight in time. Meanwhile, here in Nahalal, there is a magnificent little avenue of palm trees leading up to a statue whose purpose I could not decipher from its Hebrew inscription, and some fairly big and fine buildings, such as a synagogue, a school, etc. After realizing that there was no time left to push on to Afula, which lies to the southeast of Nahalal at the base of the hills opposite Hazorea, I turned back to the Kfar Yehoshua track and arrived home very late for lunch.

February 28

Talking to one of the recently arrived Americans at breakfast, I found he was quite familiar with London and knew Leadenhall Street, in and near which I had worked in shipping offices for so many years. A reception for the Americans was held in the dining hall after supper. Nothing special happened: the Secretary made a speech of welcome which was translated into English, paragraph by paragraph, by a member who seems to act as semiofficial translator-interpreter. There were a few songs by our choir, a few cookies to eat, and the American girl who was evidently senior in the group as regards knowledge of Hebrew, made a perfectly successful reply in that language, which was not translated. Perhaps her companions had learned its substance from her beforehand; for me, however, it was too difficult to understand.

March 1

When I called for my mail today at the post-office hut,
after seeing my name in the Hebrew list on the bulletin
board, I found that the German woman who handled the
mail had an assistant. She handed my letter, which she took
out of the tray, to a little girl of, perhaps, five, who
solemnly passed it across the counter to me.

March 4

I set out for a walk to **Sarid,** the kibbutz almost due east
of Hazorea, where a Uruguayan friend I met on my boat
was settled. However, all my efforts to find the correct path
across the Emek were unavailing. Paths insisted on peter-
ing out into orchards, rubbish heaps—anything. Drifting
farther and farther south, down the main road, past Mishmar Haemek, I eventually came within range of Megiddo,
and decided to go there and see its famous ruins instead.
The great mound, the size of a handsome small hill, and
not unduly small at that, was lots of trouble to climb from
the road. The round trip Hazorea-Megiddo was a good ten
miles, but it certainly was worth it. On top was a whole
maze of uncovered foundations, ruins of ancient walls, pil-
lars, and arches, just like the pictures in the archaeology
books. Archaeology is not my subject; I prefer geology, to
get literally down to bedrock; but there was no denying
the interest, indeed the romance, of the scene. I was completely alone there as I wandered in the labyrinth of ruins
from ancient days and looked over the Emek on one side,
and the rolling hills at the back, which appeared in very
different formation from the Hazorea setting. I wonder
whether someone will be walking across the remains of
Hazorea in a few thousand years' time similarly thinking
of the strange panorama of human history. But I hope

Hazorea will have a better story to tell in the future than the sorry tale of fighting and destruction revealed in the Megiddo strata of the past.

I continued on, past the ruins of the Arab village of Lajun, to the crossroads dominated by the so-called police station, a comparatively large building in cream-colored concrete of standard pattern—one finds such buildings at strategic points all over the country, I am told. They are, of course, not at all police stations in the English sense of the phrase, but actually fortresses. It seems that nearby Megiddo really owed its importance to the highways crossing nearby, whatever they were called in pre-Biblical, Biblical, and post-Biblical days. It is located at the spot where the only practicable road from the coastal plain issues out of the Wadi Ara in a southwest-northeast direction towards Afula and Lake Tiberias beyond, and crosses at right angles the route which follows the southwestern edge of the Emek in a northwest-southeast direction and connects Haifa Bay with the hills of Samaria. I decided to continue on this latter road and to get as near the Jordan frontier as I safely could. I hoped I could at least see the frontier post from the distance. Another mile or so brought me to the kibbutz of Givat Oz ("Hill of Strength"—the hill is insignificant and I do not know about the strength). Beyond it I came across a notice saying something about the enemy at two kilometers, but there was still no sign of any actual frontier post. So I walked over the bar carrying the notice and tentatively began a few yards' further exploration. But I was soon waved back by a kibbutznik who jumped out of the Givat Oz cowyard; he cried out something about frontier, for which I knew the Hebrew word, so I understood that one was not permitted to go any farther, even on foot. Later on I heard it was unsafe to pro-

ceed on the road beyond Givat Oz; the additional two kilometers may seem a lot, but, in these times of armistice a
no-man's land of this width is certainly necessary. This
means that some eight miles down from Hazorea is as far
as one can go now along the main road to the southeast.

From a rise in the road outside the Givat Oz fence I
could see a short distance ahead. The country was, of
course, no different from that all round, but the knowledge
that somewhere on top of the nearby hills it already belonged to the Hashemite Kingdom of Jordan was certainly
interesting. Not as if one had to go to Givat Oz to see Jordan; similar foreign hills are visible from Hazorea itself in
that direction except on really hazy days. Incidentally, I
heard that before the establishment of Israel a line of the
Egged bus cooperative used to operate down our road connecting Haifa and Jerusalem via Jenin, Nablus, and
Ramallah. This was, in fact, the regular direct route between the two cities. I wonder if it will be restored as an
international bus service when peace eventually comes
about.

On returning to the Lajun crossroads, I had to wait about
three-quarters of an hour, with a Yemenite family, with
whom I could barely exchange a word or two of Hebrew,
before I got a "tramp," that is, a lift, back to Hazorea. There were plenty of trucks passing, but they would
not stop.

All in all, it was an interesting morning trip, and all by
mistake. For if I could have got on the early morning bus
direct from Hazorea to Tiberias, I would have explored
the romantic Jordan Valley instead. I shall have to do that
as soon as possible, in any case, but it is evidently hopeless
to try to get on the bus down here. The only thing to do is
to go into Haifa and board the bus there at its starting

point. Then, one can go through Nazareth, bypassing
Hazorea altogether, and later return to Hazorea directly,
thus making a convenient circular tour. That, I hope, is
for the immediate future. But today's failures, first with
Tiberias and then with Sarid, which will also have to be
tackled again soon, certainly led me to plenty of places of
interest not far from home.

March 6

There was only a short spell of milking today, so far as
I was concerned; the hour or two I used to devote to
this activity after coming home from the pasture is a thing
of the past. I still take far too long over each sheep: five
minutes instead of two. But it is only a matter of practice
—I hope.

I have competitors at pasture every day now. A flock—
sorry: herd—of cows comes up a side valley from
Yoqneam and occupies much of my grazing ground. I am
told it is permitted, so I quite literally move to pastures
new. After all, there is plenty of room on the hills, although
the good-quality rough grass, if one can use such contradic-
tory terms, is more limited.

March 9

One of the Americans asked me this morning how it
was I knew English so well! It having been my native language for some thirty-four years now, I am not personally
puzzled by this phenomenon. But as I am the only inhabit-
ant of actual English origin in Hazorea, I can quite understand it seeming unusual. I am now beginning to work
with the Americans, and with the two English girls—I
forgot they were also in Hazorea when I wrote what I did
just now; but they are only temporaries for the six months'

seminar. At last it looks as though I am leaving the sheep for a time and transferring to the vegetable gardens, just picking cauliflowers and things like that. The quantities involved, however, are very large. The Americans work half a day, only, and the regulars carry on for the rest of the time.

March 16

Not only have I got to know an American clarinetist from New York who has turned up here and who helps, most inappropriately, with the cauliflowers, but I have also been introduced to his most admirable kitten. We have enjoyable times in my hut discussing music, and the kitten has even been lent to me for an overnight stay!

March 18

This was certainly the most remarkable day I have spent since I arrived in Asia. The reason, I think, lay in the atmosphere, both physical and social, for both were quite different from anything I had previously experienced. This time, I actually did get to Tiberias—and beyond—but things began very badly and I nearly gave up before I properly started. The start, in fact, took quite five hours. I had heard that there were early morning trucks from Hazorea to Haifa every hour from 5 A.M. onwards, so I got up by 4:30 and prowled around looking for one. But there was nothing. The same later. Finally, I went back to sleep but was up in time to get on the regular milk truck at 7. With an optimism quite unusual for me, I asked to be put down at the road junction for Tiberias, less than half-way from Hazorea to Haifa, in the hope that the early morning bus from the city would stop there and take me through Nazareth to Tiberias by 9 or so. But, of course, in spite of the fact that there were two relief buses, none stopped at the road junction. I decided to walk to Nesher, where the famous cement works are, and there take the suburban bus to Haifa. As it happened, a truck picked me up soon after I started to walk, which was a good thing, for the distance was much greater than I had thought. Dropped at the cement works, I still had quite a walk to the outer suburban bus terminal; however, I got into the city soon after 8 and I expected to manage the 8:30 Tiberias bus all right. However, my troubles were far from over. When I reached the bus station in Haifa, I was given a ticket marked "9:30." The 8:30 bus had been fully booked, and the 9:30 would not reach Tiberias till nearly midday. Was it worth going so late? After finding that I could not reach the ancient city of Safed (which was also on my list of "musts") any earlier, I decided it was and duly waited. I spent the remaining time reading a Penguin book on Roman Britain, which I had noticed and bought in the nearby bookstore. The 9:30 bus drifted off about a quarter of an hour late, but the ride turned out to be so magnificent that I completely forgot to worry about the time.

The long climb toward Nazareth was unexciting, but Nazareth itself turned out to be a fascinating place as the bus wound its way down into it. The quaint old stone houses, the orange stalls every few yards, and the traditionally dressed Arabs everywhere were an entirely new and very impressive sight for me. I was most surprised at the general disjointedness of the place: even the central bus stop seemed to be in a mere alley at the back of miscellaneous one-story buildings containing small stores and shops, and no part of the town seemed to be any more definite in shape. Then the bus climbed out of the town's large hollow, snaking fast up the hillside, and was soon

on a rolling plateau where Arabs tilled their fields and the
land rose and fell in all directions in a dissected jumble.
After quite a long time, the hill country ended ahead:
there was a turn, a dip, and then—the Sea of Galilee or
Lake Kinneret, as its Hebrew name goes, gleaming below.
The road wound down to it very steeply, first to the upper
outskirts of Tiberias town, with pleasant streets of beautiful suburban villas, garlanded with flowers and looking
out over the lake. A minute or so later we were in the lower
town, ancient Tiberias itself. It is a disappointingly dirty
and disheveled city, although one of the most important
in the land. It was a quarter to twelve when the bus finished up rather vaguely in the main street. I had a short
walk along the small waterfront with a fishing flavor, quite
unimportant, such as one finds at very small West Country
ports in England, but without their charm.

As soon as possible I took a further bus, meaning to visit
famous Degania, mother of the kibbutzim, founded in
1909. This ride had an interest of its own, the road going
past the hot springs, where there is a considerable bathing
establishment along the edge of the water. I was particularly interested, of course, to see a flock of sheep, standing very foolishly in the hot sun on the pebbles at the lake-
side, when by moving a few yards down the road they could
have been on rough herbage under the shade of trees. The
Kinneret sheep seem to be even sillier than those of
Hazorea!

I was very eager to see the place where the River Jordan
flows out of the lake, but did not know where to get off
the bus. Soon, the road left the lake shore and went over a
bridge which evidently crossed the Jordan itself. Thus I
went right past Degania and landed up at the kibbutz
Afikim, which, however, I also wanted to see very much.

For it was from a booklet about this very kibbutz Afikim, which I had obtained in England by mail from Jerusalem, that I had learned most of what I knew about kibbutz life prior to my arrival in Israel.

And Afikim did not disappoint in the least. When I saw its size, I wondered that so many people could live successfully and work in the peculiarly thick and hot atmosphere of the Jordan Valley. This being mid-March, I tried to imagine how hot and stifling it must be in the summer. At any rate, the climate did not seem to worry the Afikimites. They had a tremendous plywood factory in their front gateway; it was so huge that, in comparison, the Hazorea carpentry appeared like a toy shop. But the most fascinating thing of all for me was to see bananas growing. I felt I was in the middle of darkest Africa, at least! There were plantations at the back and plantations across the road in front. To my amazement, I found that the banana plant grows huge, dark red flowers: I am not sure whether they ever open properly, as they seem to turn straight from buds into baby bananas. Perhaps I arrived at the wrong time of the season, though. Some of the young "hands" were wrapped up in sacking: I am not quite sure why. Nor am I quite sure whether to call the banana plants bushes or trees: with their giant leaves, some are as tall as trees, but others are junior, or perhaps "dwarf" strains.

The dining hall at Afikim is a very fine affair, with magnificent doors fit for a concert hall. Electric fans are fitted —very necessary in the Jordan Valley climate. Outside are beautiful gardens, lawns, trees, seats. When I left the place, after exploring it quite thoroughly, I had a look at the narrow-gauge railway which used to connect Haifa and Damascus and which runs down the Emek, past Hazorea at Kfar Yehoshua, then turns round north up the Jordan to

Afikim and the Syrian border beyond on the east. All I found of it was a length of rail of about one yard, apparently left as a souvenir, at Afikim's main doorway: the line originally ran at the side of the road, in front of the Afikim wire fence. I understand it will never be restored, and certainly not as a narrow-gauge line.

The bus back took me to Degania in a few minutes, rushing up the Jordan Valley main road. I did not like the scenery as much as at Hazorea. The mountains on the Syrian side are grim, squat, and furrowed: and those on the other side are in no way special. Degania itself, split into two as a result of its growth, was quite easy to inspect. I walked through part of Degania A and continued past an orange grove. I wondered why so much of the Jordan Valley air seemed scented, as the Afikim bananas had no smell, but I now realized that the orange blossoms were responsible for it. The buildings I reached beyond the grove turned out to belong to Degania B. Although more than a decade younger than Degania A, this kibbutz, too, is among the oldest in the land. It was the first I had seen to look really finished. With no signs of building going on, the gardens, lawns, and houses all seemed to be in almost complete, tidy order; with big trees nearly everywhere, the effect was truly beautiful and gracious. Curiously, Degania A did not strike me as being nearly so well ordered. However, I may have missed its best parts, or it may have other work requirements or different land-usage needs. I had a very brief glimpse at the inside of the small, natural history musuem of Degania A, but, natural history never having been a subject of mine, it did not interest me too much. There was no time left to look for the Jordan running through Degania's fields; actually, the Jordan separates Degania from Kibbutz Kinneret on the opposite bank. Before the next hourly bus came along, however, I had time to inspect the junction of the river and the lake at one end of the bridge over which the buses speed. The river flows out at an outrageous angle, very slowly indeed, it seems. Incidentally, the Jordan Valley kibbutzim use open concrete irrigation channels instead of pipes as in the Emek: cheaper, no doubt, but wasteful on account of evaporation. Little steps are put up every now and then, so that paths can continue across the channels.

The bus made a good start on the short run back into Tiberias: it collided slightly with a truck at the lake-junction end of the Jordan bridge. No doubt it was the truck driver's fault. He had a hilarious gang of youngsters on board; after a slight argument, we proceeded in good order. This was the last bus to connect with the direct one back from Tiberias to Hazorea. There was a longish wait in the main street, and I overheard some Spanish being spoken, apart, of course, from Hebrew. I managed, as usual, quite well with my mixture of Hebrew and English; my Spanish is of little use outside Hazorea, where I am in close contact with the few who know it. Not unexpectedly, the driver of the Hazorea bus, when it came in, was our own long-distance man, so that I was driven home once again by one of our own members. He had to take the bus to the terminal at Haifa and return later in the evening.

As we climbed up towards the lofty plateau which has to be crossed in order to reach my part of the country, I noticed a sign at the side of the road which I had not seen on the outward journey. It said "Sea Level" in Hebrew and French. I have no idea why French was added to the Hebrew, but for me it was an asset, as I could not read the Hebrew. Looking back, I realized the immensity of the Jordan depression, which surrounds the Sea of Galilee. More than ever one felt like having visited another world—a virtually subterranean one! The "other world" impression must, of course, be mainly subjective; yet the thick, hot air, the bananas, the irrigation channels, the Yemenites chanting their queer songs in the bus—all these things went a long way towards building up the effect of having been to another Israel, a world of its own, much more a part of the Arab Middle East than the environs of Hazorea.

Once out of the Jordan depression I felt comparatively at home again. In order to head for Afula and Hazorea, the bus turned off the road it had traveled and struck out at a different angle, skirting the very foot of Mount Tabor, so prominent in the Hazorea view. Every possible scrap of land seemed to be cultivated—and the "scraps" rolled on, mile after mile. The grain production of this region alone must be formidable, as one settlement after another adds its produce. The bus, driven with great skill at high speed, took me for the first time into the bus station of Afula, a busy market town which, however, never grew as its founders intended. It is a slightly haphazard jumble of modernity, apart from its overpompous avenue of palms. And, before 7 P.M., my minimum program splendidly completed, I was back at the main gate of Hazorea, greatly enriched in experience. One of the ways in which I was enriched turned out to be the quantity of dust I had accumulated, as was evident on return. I had been treated to quite a good specimen of a dust storm between leaving Degania and getting into the homebound bus at Tiberias. After the sky got quite dark, a strong wind arose, and although there was no question of being immersed in swirling dust or anything like that, there was so much blowing about that it became quite inconvenient, and plenty of traces remained on me when I got indoors. Further evidence of having visited a strange land was thus provided not only mentally but physically.

March 19

For the first time, I worked in the building department. The work was extremely elementary, consisting of filling buckets with small pebbles and passing them over to the men who tipped them into the concrete mixer along with the sand, cement, and water which other of my colleagues provided similarly. My job was done with a turiah—the L-shaped spade which, I now find, has its blade bent at more than a right angle to the handle. I really should not say bent, for the blade is straight lengthwise although slightly curved across its width. This was hard work, and it went on for a day and a quarter, i.e., an extra couple of hours beyond the normal nine, for some special scheduling reasons. We were building a grain store on to the front of the huge new chicken house. The concrete was poured into the wooden mold as we and the mixing machine got it ready. For this job, our own building people were supplemented by hired workers who spoke only German or Yiddish, so that communicationwise I was worse off than ever. But we had a specially nice tea with cakes before doing the extra evening shift.

Later, I again noticed the extraordinary luminosity which gleams over the Carmel and the hills behind the meshek, as the sun, long sunk below their tops, still irradiated the deep twilight just above the outline of the ridges. I have never seen a comparable effect in England, although I would hesitate to say that it is a Mediterranean specialty. And as I turned from admiring this beautiful effect in the west to go into my room, the electric light promptly failed, and it was necessary to play about with a candle for twenty minutes until the Haifa power station got going again.

March 20

Contacting my American clarinetist friend again, I was invited to look in on his late-evening practice session after my Hebrew lesson. The Hebrew lesson, as a matter of fact, did not quite come off. Talking about the clarinetist's cat led to talking about other things in English and that was as far as we got that day. But there were important things to be said, especially that cats faced very brief lives in Hazorea, because whenever the necessary rat poison was periodically and professionally distributed around the place, cats inevitably tended to eat poisoned rats or mice, with fatal effects. Considerable concern was aroused for the future of Shoshana, the American kitten so valued by the clarinetist and myself, but it was decided that Shoshana should remain at Hazorea under my care while her owner made an exploratory trip to Tel Aviv and Jerusalem for a few weeks. I could not think of any other suitable Hebrew name for Shoshana, and since cats with their supergraceful movements are Mozartean creatures anyway, the name of a character from *Figaro* seemed just right and it gained the approval of her master.

The clarinetist's practice session produced some very beautiful sounds afterwards. He had obtained permission to use the hillside dugout (a solidly constructed brick room, half concealed in the hillside, which dates back to the Arab-Israeli war days). Others, too, utilized this room: twice a week it was occupied by our visiting dentist from Yoqneam for whose purpose it was very well fitted up until such time as the dentist could get a proper room of his own in the new medical block. I heard that one of our artists also, used it, and I was delighted to be allowed to go through a large pile of his latest productions which lay on the floor. Thus, there were remarkably artistic goings on this evening, what with the clarinet pieces of Mozart and Brahms, and the collection of striking modern paintings, among the drills, chemicals, and other equipment of the dentist.

March 22

According to the work schedule, I was supposed to do a spell in the culture department today; instead, I spent most of the day in general yard work, and then I was put to work on the manure heap for a short time. There are times when the huge work sheets in their frames in the dining room go slightly astray in the information they schedule! I wonder if they are ver corrected for final statistical purposes, or whether I shall always stand in the records as having done a period of cultural work this afternoon.

The dining room, incidentally, was quite a sight with the Purim decorations up on the walls. Cardboard figures caricaturing members of the kibbutz, among other items of great variety, including a delightful representation of our moshavnik dressed as a Chinaman (since he had come from Manchuria) leading a couple of sheep! At least one of our artists had obviously let loose with a vengeance and had thoroughly enjoyed himself with cardboard and paint. The youth group held its Purim party in the evening and had a fine time with folk dancing to the music of piano, violin, and tambourine.

March 23

While working under the guidance of one of our finest agricultural experts this afternoon, and playing a very minor part in the repair of one of our irrigation pipelines, I was told by him that crops were ready in this country two or three months earlier than in England, owing to the warmer weather. The temperature range now is between 53° F. and 73° F., which is certainly above English averages for the third week in March. I had not realized that there was such a marked difference.

This evening was the turn of the adults to have their Purim party. I have never seen anything like it, and I certainly never thought Hazorea could produce anything so astonishing. About a hundred members dressed up in costumes of incredible variety and complexity. They represented, among items ranging from rabbis to Chinamen, what seemed to me practically all the picturesque characters of the English countryside, although, I suppose, they really were meant to be characters from the German countryside. The two are after all not so utterly dissimilar. I understand that the parents of members lent all sorts of old dresses, thereby making the remarkable display possible. The evening was partly taken up with humorous sketches performed on a temporary stage in the dining room. Many of those in fancy dress took part, and, although I could not understand much of what was going on, I could certainly see the fun of such sketches as those involving the ludicrous interviewing of candidates for admission to the kibbutz, and so on. Eventually, dancing began on a grand scale. In the hope of seeing the end, as a matter of interest, I stayed up till twenty of three in the morning, and then gave it up as a bad job. I gathered afterwards that the dance went on till half-past three, not that many people were left by that time. Purim is such a quiet minor festival in English Jewry for the most part that although I had vaguely heard of its carnival aspect, I never dreamt of anything like this. Evidently it is the one night in the year when Hazorea really goes gay on an outrageously successful scale. It is a good thing the following day is Shabbat, so that workers can duly recover!

March 24

Taking plenty of time to recover, I did not set out on my Shabbat walk until four in the afternoon, when I took the path which leads up to the monastery on top of Mount Carmel. The path, a very steep affair in places, with Arabs or Druzes coming down on donkeys occasionally, led on to a surprisingly fine, broad track after about an hour's climb, and, the monastery not being in sight, I turned right, in what I thought was the correct direction. Magnificent views of the coastal plain and the sea far off opened up before me. One was in quite a different world up here on top of Carmel, although so near to Hazorea. On the way up, the whole Emek had been spread out below like a great patchwork quilt of fields, with the mountains on the other side seen from a fresh angle, looking very new and different. Upon reaching the top, one was at times cut off entirely from any view of the ordinary world below. The effect was similar to that of being among high Alpine meadows, except that the scenery here is not at all Alpine, but composed of rocky shrubs and tiny fields cultivated at an immense expenditure of labor.

Glancing back, I found to my annoyance that I was walking away from the monastery, instead of towards it! It was on another spur, behind me! The daylight was now beginning to fade, and I doubted whether I could reach the monastery and get down again to the civilized world by dark. I turned back, and, making the best speed possible, proceeded along the main track in this opposite direction, until I came to a point where it turned sharply uphill to the monastery itself, just above. By then, there was no time to complete the journey. I found a small path leading down, which I hoped would be roughly parallel with my first one. So it was, at first; but then it swung round towards the sea and, after yielding me splendid hillside views of sweeping majesty across the Emek, started to lead me towards the coastal plain. I eventually had to abandon the path and cut across the rough hillside. As the light gradually faded, I worked my way down over the rocky ground, once or twice having to resort to elementary rock traversing. Towards the end of my descent I had to resort to my flashlight. At one time I found myself too near the edge of a quarry, so that I had to retrace my steps. Finally I got down to the road and set out for the straight walk home.

March 25

We had another sheep feast in the evening, for which occasion a few lambs had been killed. If the results did not taste quite so perfect as last time, they were still quite outstanding and it was a fine affair for us shepherds.

March 30

I was just in time after work to hear my clarinetist friend broadcast in a recorded program from Jerusalem. Very smoothly it went, too.

It had been a queer day in one respect. When I looked across to the Galilee hills, I could not recognize them at all. I had to look again, to make sure I was seeing the right things. I was, and I wasn't. For it was just hazy enough to cut out the Upper Galilee hills almost entirely, leaving those of the Lower Galilee standing out in front, virtually on their own. Normally they shade into the higher ones behind, but this time they stood out isolated, creating a different outline. I was quite puzzled until I realized what was happening.

In the evening, a large chorus and small orchestra of high-school kids from Mishmar Haemek came to give us a concert in our dining hall. Except that the orchestra could not quite manage a difficult piece of Bach counterpoint, it went off very well, and we were all very pleased with the efforts of the youth from down the road.

March 31

For my Shabbat walk, I tackled our second nearest kibbutz: Ramat Hashofet, only a kilometer or two farther than Mishmar Haemek, up in the hills, and slightly farther than our sheep are allowed to go. It took just over an hour to reach it and, although not specially impressive, it turned out to be a pleasant place to walk around. From its playing field it was just possible to see the sea, straight across in the west; but Ramat Hashofet is too involved in its own hilly plateau to have very commanding views either towards the sea or towards the Emek. The most important feature of the place turned out to be the dining hall, a finely designed structure of corrugated sheeting, concrete, and wood. I never imagined that these diverse materials could be used with such pleasant results. I understand the structure is quite recent; the interior is very well done in wood, and the building is quite a credit to the place. I particularly noticed little covered litter boxes on posts everywhere around. We certainly could do with them at Hazorea to replace our old tin bins.

On my return, the clarinetist was waiting for me. He had almost obtained certain jobs, and would shortly leave for good to confirm them. Meanwhile, we were worried about Shoshana, for the beautiful little cat had been missing for several days!

April 2

I plowed onions this afternoon—that is, I led the horse, while an expert guided the little plowshare which turned up the earth between the lines of plants in a huge field behind the last houses of the meshek and up the wadi leading into the hills. In an interval I asked my companion what the stonework visible nearby was. Quite casually he answered that it was a Roman mill. I was struck by the difference in timescale to which people are used here, as compared with England. In a Biblical country, Roman ruins belong to the recent past, and are taken quite as a matter of course. When I heard what the ruins at the edge of the wadi were, I remembered the spring in the rocks at the side of the main path where the sheep usually drink when I lead them past: it is usually referred to as a Roman well. Apparently, it is assumed that the Romans cut the rocks into convenient shapes around it. There is now a little rock basin there, although I do not know whether that too is meant to be their handiwork. A tiny stream runs from the spot, crosses the end of the onion field, and falls into the wadi.

A child brought the deplorable news to the clarinetist that he had seen Shoshana dead after she had eaten a poisoned mouse. This must be one of the most horrible tragedies that has ever befallen Hazorea. I am told that a red note is pinned on the bulletin board each time prior to the distribution of the rat poison, but all agree that there was no such notice this time. How Shoshana could have found a mouse poisoned weeks ago is a hopeless mystery. My intention had been to tie her on a very long string to a tree outside my hut during the day on which the poison was put down; but, as soon as I did this, someone released her, obviously because he regarded this as too cruel. Now Shoshana will never again be able to eat her little dishes of soup and fish on my doorstep.

April 3

Today I constructed a little chicken run for some of the children outside their house. They were highly critical of my work, but in the end they approved it and moved their chickens into the new home. Incidentally, the temperature midday was 77° in the shade and 114° in the sun.

April 4

My work certainly becomes more varied now that I am emancipated from the sheep in earnest. Today's job was to clean out a choked and silted-up ditch which runs along the side of the road just outside our fence and discharges into the wadi under the main road. I had to clear the weeds and widen the channel in the earth so that the waste water from our laundry could run down freely. It was quite a fascinating job. Playing with water like this is one of the nicest jobs I know, in fact.

April 6

The temperature is fifteen degrees cooler all of a sudden, so we are down to English levels for early April. There was a sudden change of wind after my Hebrew lesson last night. I think it must have switched from east to west and started blowing gustily about.

April 11

On the third attempt this evening I actually succeeded in getting up to Hazorea's little hillside cemetery. My Irish friend has told me he had been working hard during the day digging a grave for someone's parent who had just died and was going to be buried here although he had lived in Haifa. Twice previously I had taken the wrong path. Now I learned that it was farther over, by the swimming pool, and I made the right approach up a zigzag avenue of cypresses and found the few rows of very plain tombstones, about twenty in all, and inscribed mostly with nothing but names and dates. Only the one or two stones of war casualties had fuller details. The little cemetery, something like ten minutes' slow walk uphill, is situated very beautifully, with a view right up the valley out to the sea north of Haifa Bay in a final glimpse between the hills in the distance.

On the way down I was most amused to come across a little girl squatting cross-legged on the patch of lawn outside her parents' room, and carefully practicing the recorder with a children's Hebrew book of recorder music on the grass in front of her. The recorder, descended from the Arab flute or whatever it was originally, is, I understand, the national instrument of Israel. Being inexpensive and made locally, children learn to play it as a matter of course in school, and use it in quaintly squeaky orchestras with percussion. The head shepherd once told me that even the wildest children have been tamed by the self-control necessary for playing the recorder, which thus has great educational value.

April 29

This week I am continuing my long spell of grain work, bagging the grain at the elevator, tying the sacks, and helping to load them for storage. Variety is assured by frequent sessions of mixing a ton of chicken feed at a time in the main storehouse. One collects sacks of barley, fishmeal, bran, and various other feeds in a miniature mountain in the middle of the concrete floor, turns it over twice with spades, and rebags the duly assorted result for transit to the chicken houses just as for the sheep. Certain grades of chickens also get powdered milk, from Canada or the U.S.A., mixed in, and the young chicks receive Icelandic cod liver oil also. The latter is a great nuisance, as it has to be poured out of its large can onto a heap of bran, mixed, and then rubbed through a sieve so that the bran become fairly branlike again and can be mixed in with the other ingredients. One usually finishes off these mixtures with several pounds of salt. My Irish friend has learned so much about the mixing technique that now usually he himself gets hold of the ingredients from all around the store, following the list of varieties and weights provided. As I was going to supper in the dining room I saw a lot of low, white shapes moving in the same direction in the dark. The sheep had again done the impossible: they had escaped, and were apparently also aiming at supper in the dining room! I instantaneously jumped into the breach, and started swishing them back home. I don't know whether they knew they were doing wrong, but they turned back towards their adjacent home without stopping to eat the sparse grass growing on the way. The moshavnik turned up by chance a minute or two later, and helped me finish putting the animals away. No one, he said, could have left the gates open, but we know that it is not absolutely impossible for an enterprising sheep to lift a latch with its horns if it juggles patiently enough. This is what seems to have happened this time. We used to secure the latches with ropes, but this precaution has been neglected of late. At any rate, with some delay we managed to sit down to supper without the company of the sheep in the dining room.

April 30

The character of the work at the grain elevator has changed somewhat. The barley harvest, already threshed by machine, is coming in from the fields in trucks which dump the grain into bins at the base of the elevator. The job is to help with this operation, and, after the grain has been passed through the cleaning machine, to bag it. The course taken by the grain before it gets into the sacks is, to say the least, extraordinary. First, it goes through certain pipes to the cleaning machine, which is a very clever device: an electrically driven fan drives a current of air through the falling grain so that lightweight impurities fall through a wire mesh when the grain subsequently is passed over shaking trays. Then it goes many yards up into the storage bins (capacity about thirty tons), carried up on a moving belt of pockets or miniature buckets. Following this it falls by gravity through the outflow pipes straight into the sacks we hold underneath. We are having a new and much improved grain-cleaning machine installed now, and also a mixing machine for chicken and other animal foods, so much progress is afoot.

May 5

After two days of clearing out a chicken house, a very tame job of scraping floors and cleaning wire netting, things livened up today with sheep shearing. My part in the proceedings was very indefinite at first, but it grew livelier quite rapidly. I was supposed merely to pile up the fleece as cut, but I was soon involved in much more than just this. I had to help catch the sheep, tie up their legs, pick them up, and put them on the shearing tables (rough wooden affairs collected from goodness knows where), lift them off afterwards, untie their legs on the floor, and release them through a typically ramshackle gate in the hurdling which set apart a section of the sheep shed for shearing purposes. It was a highly diverting job, if a trifle hectic at times, since the sheep had all sorts of ideas about how to behave, most of them unsuitable. We had various extra people brought in from other departments to help the shepherds on the job. Two electric clippers were in use, just like barbers' clippers but on a bigger scale; also about five pairs of simple-looking sheep clippers or shears, which, however, worked quite all right. I had a snip or two at an unfortunate animal myself when no one was looking later on and it seemed quite easy, but our moshavnik who practiced a little afterwards, said it was quite difficult to cut the sheep's fat tails, which now could be seen for the first time in their proper shape. These tails come in three parts: two bulging side pieces hanging down a little, and in the middle a little curled up twist, like a pig's tail. It is getting around the latter without puncturing the poor sheep's skin which is so difficult. When the sheep did get cut—and sometimes, when the shearers went wrong, they had quite a few cuts all over them—an additional part of my job was to dab their cuts with tar (which, much to their annoyance, is also put on their noses and ears to stop skin scabs). This was no doubt the equivalent of treating a human cut with iodine, but the sheep took it more passively than most humans do.

May 6

The shearing of some of the lambs was postponed until tomorrow. Their wool is too short to come off in one piece, so it is clipped off in little lumps, unlike that of the sheep. Nevertheless, the third and last mutton feast of the season was held for the shearers at teatime today. I myself was out at pasture with the shorn animals and the few not yet done, but when I returned I was most appreciatively surprised to find a huge lump of excellent cold lamb waiting in my room. Really most kind of those concerned.

May 7

In the afternoons, after the midday milking, the sheep now go to a roadside field of corn, grown specially for them, with which they are extremely pleased. But today they decided to play around on the way, although the distance is less than a mile down the road. First they stopped to graze by the roadside on the right; then some of them became bold enough to try what is absolutely forbidden: break into a field of alfalfa on the left. I had to run around more or less at once on both sides of the road, and to collect them together again, with heavy trucks thundering by every few minutes. At certain periods, I had to leave part of the flock in the middle of the road to look after themselves, hoping that the truck drivers would avoid them as best they could, while I was chasing another group out of the alfalfa. Eventually, and almost to my surprise, the various sections became united again and we were able to proceed in the correct manner. The sheep seem to have shrunk to a fraction of their normal size, now that their wool is off, and they all look extremely small. The lambs, now about three-quarter size after only half a year, look particularly silly, because, for some reason or other, their legs were not shorn, and they look as though they are wearing thick, shaggy socks all the way up. The flock can now fairly easily be separated into milking and non-milking sections according to their paint marks, and therefore all of them are taken out together, some four hundred head. They must make an impressively amusing picture trotting along the road after me. They insist on spreading out over the whole width of the road: so much the worse for any wheeled traffic which tries to get in the way. With their long brown ears flapping madly and their heads bobbing up and down, they move along like a wave of wool, looking, I hope, at least as ridiculous to me as I, leading them, no doubt look to them.

May 9

Having my Shabbat in the middle of the week instead of at the end, I was able to take part this morning in a lorry trip to the Lower Galilee mountains. I was, of course, the only tourist passenger. After an incredibly bumpy ride along minor roads, during which I was continually being hurled up from the floor of the truck, we reached the main road from Acre to Safed and followed it for some distance. We eventually arrived at the quarry, from which a special reddish-yellow stone is obtained in slabs, suitable for paving certain areas around our House of Culture, now nearing completion.

On the way we passed plenty of Arabs, the Galilee having the greatest concentration of Arabs in Israel. Some of them rode on camels or drove the heavily laden "ships of the desert," trotting behind them. The scenery was no more striking than that of Carmel, but it was all new to me, first of a rolling, then a rugged, type. Loading our lorry with the stone was an extremely leisurely business, and I had plenty of time to walk around. The Arab quarrymen shared some of their late breakfast with us. Their bread was quite nice, but I could not make much of their unspecified-vegetable rolls, which seemed tasteless. On the way back, we took a different route, keeping to main roads all the way, perhaps because of our heavy load. We skirted Acre, but, looking back as we sped along the coast road toward Haifa, I had a fine view of this picturesque old harbor town. We also bypassed Haifa itself, but when we stopped at a cafe on the way I saw a good many trucks decorated with posters for tomorrow's Independence Day.

May 10

I could not go to the Haifa celebrations of Independence Day, as I was on duty with the sheep for half the day. Actually, it was a three-quarters holiday at Hazorea, work being done only for quarter of a day. But since one cannot take the sheep to pasture for so short a time, it was arranged that I should get back my two-and-a-quarter hours some time later on.

Incidentally, I have started wearing shorts again, for the first time since I was a child. They are quite ubiquitous in this country, but only in the summer, from April or May. I should have thought the climate was hot enough to wear them in the winter too, like the customs officers. Even in the summer not everybody uses them, but now they are becoming quite usual, for both work and off-duty time. They are, of course, much cooler than long trousers, but one's legs get very sunburnt at first.

May 12

I set out early on this Shabbat morning on my third attempt to reach the monastery on top of Mount Carmel. This time I turned up too far around its back, but nevertheless I proceeded up the track which, according to the map, winds along the summit of Carmel into Haifa—a matter of over ten miles, no doubt. All went well for a time, although I seemed to take a long while—four hours—to reach the Druse village of Dalyat-el-Karmil. When I asked them the way, they preferred English to Hebrew—my Hebrew, at any case.

After Dalyat the path became very rough, and wound up hills and down into little internal rocky gulleys with picturesque Druses cultivating their dubious patches. By mid-afternoon I wound up in a valley head from which it was most difficult to climb out. The actual track swept round towards the sea, so I had to leave it or, I thought, I would never reach Haifa. Eventually, working my way up old Arab earth-retaining walls across the valley, I found an army camp on top, where they directed me along the fine motor road outside. When I finally reached Haifa's municipal boundaries, I only just about managed to take a local bus down into the center of the city in time to connect with the early evening bus home to Hazorea.

The walk had taken me ten hours, including two spent resting. Apart from the fine Carmel scenery itself, Dalyat village had provided the focal point of the day. Only near Limassol, Cyprus, had I seen such a typically Middle Eastern village before. With its largish, square stone houses, flat roofs, open-fronted shops and little alleyways, with the dignified Druses walking about in its streets, it was a really picturesque place, only a few miles from Hazorea. It was here that I had my first *gazoz,* said to be the national drink of Israel—an only slightly fizzy lemonade or other fruit drink: not too bad.

May 13

The time has come to take my five days' "immigration holiday," to which new immigrants to a kibbutz are entitled after getting reasonably settled. I left Hazorea for Tel Aviv just before 5 A.M. in a truck which dropped me on the outskirts of the city. It took me three-quarters of an hour, in addition to the interesting two hours' ride through the Hills of Ephraim and down a long stretch of the coastal plain past Hedera, to get into the city itself on a local rush-hour bus. Although the famous central bus station is quite good, with its half-dozen or so bays and platforms, it is far too small for its crowds of people and buses. Until the station is expanded, vehicles start off from side streets all around it as well. My first impression of the city was not favorable; it seemed to be quite a mess. Previously, I had seen it only from the sea, when it looked splendid. But I put off any proper tour for the time being, and took a further bus to Bat Yam, the farthest suburb down the coast beyond Jaffa. By mistake I got off in Jaffa—at first also, a disappointment. I wandered for a long time in drab streets, which might almost have belonged to Birmingham, although they were not unspacious. Eventually, I found Jaffa's main street, whose quaint corners near the small harbor certainly made up for the rest. Once again, I was right in the midst of the picturesque Arab world, complete with street vendors, loudspeakers in cafes blaring forth with Arabic music, and plenty of oranges. The latter seem to cost the same in Jaffa as in London! But no doubt it was the very end of the season that accounted for the high local price. Nor were they "Jaffa" oranges; they were of the small Valencia type, the season for the big ones being over.

When I got back to Tel Aviv, I soon found that its commercial center was very handsome. I made contact with a member of Kibbutz Hazorea on loan to the accounts department of the federation to which we belong. He was extremely kind, treated me to an excellent lunch in the federation's restaurant, and cleared up certain doubts I had about routes around the city. I then visited the so-called Tel Aviv Museum, which is actually a splendid, modern art gallery containing an unexpected sprinkling of French impressionists—my favorites—including even an unimportant Renoir. I spent all afternoon walking about, and gradually got a more and more complete picture of Tel Aviv. I passed famous Allenby Street, which is a fine, unpretentious shopping street; its buildings are much lower than those of London's West End. I caught a few glimpses of the northern section, which was very striking with its modern use of concrete in the architecture of the ubiquitous blocks of apartment houses. I took in the noble, curved façade of the Habimah Theater, and the remarkable effect provided by the Rothschild Boulevard, with its parallel lines of trees growing into each other to form, in some cases, a continuous wall of foliage above one's head. Tel Aviv's boulevards have garden malls in the middle which keep the opposing lines of traffic apart.

Much later in the evening than I had intended, I arrived at the nice little bungalow of my cousins, who live in a chicken-farming village a few miles out in the country. I was duly introduced to the chickens and everyone else, and was shown to an unused chicken house in which a camp bed had been set up for me. I had a most pleasant time with my cousins, whom I had not seen for many years.

May 14

I took a local bus to Petach Tikva, and had a good look at this little town. It is not really prepossessing, and while it may have a certain body and life of its own, there is no particular charm about it. The place is evidently one where private enterprise has done its little jobs without much capital and where the resultant collection of odds and ends is unimpressive although not actually unpleasant.

A bus took me from there to within some two miles' walk to Lydda airport, where I hoped to find an official who had previously lived in my very room at Hazorea before he left kibbutz life for airport work. I had been told that he had done such work in India and that it would be interesting for me to compare notes with another English immigrant. But, upon reaching the airport, I found that he had been transferred to a Tel Aviv office, and so all I could do was to have a good look around at the airport. And it really is an impressive sight. The central building, with a fine restaurant, ticket counters, and so on, could hardly be bettered. Some interesting planes were lying about, but nothing particularly exciting was going on, so I did not stay long. Passage in and out of the main gate was quite informal, once I found someone who knew English and could understand what I wanted. Outside, I was lucky enough to get a bus almost immediately, around midday, and I proceeded to Ramle via Lydda (Lod). The latter did not provide much to see—a small, Arab town, with a frowsy market square. Ramle itself, on the Tel Aviv-Jerusalem highway, was not much better, although of a fair size; apart from its dull main-street shops, I cannot tell what else it contains, for I had no time for an inspection of its back reaches, which looked duller than ever from the front. I was astonished, however, to find one or two very recent Penguin books in a shop.

Another surprise was to find that the Tel Aviv-Jerusalem buses ran every quarter of an hour. For such a long ride—about two and a half hours—this seemed to me an astoundingly good service. The mountains took on a real grandeur as the bus approached Jerusalem, while the road performed hairpin bends—and then we passed through an unimportant suburban area and were in the miserable backyard of Jerusalem's temporary bus station. It was late in the afternoon, but, living on pieces of bread and odds and ends, as I always do during my tours anywhere, I managed to walk and bus around the city a good deal before it was too late altogether, getting a very fair general impression. Almost entirely modern, Jerusalem impressed me with its small-scale self-assuredness and dignity not at all unworthy of a capital.

An early evening call at the southern district police station to see my clarinetist friend, who had joined the Jerusalem Police Band, was abortive; but later on I located him just in time to take him to a chamber concert in the beautiful auditorium of the YMCA—actually my first attendance at a public concert in Israel! The police had no objection to my using an empty bed in a room for four my friend shared, so I spent the night in a police station for the first time! Supper consisted of omelets made of egg powder cooked on an electric ring in a corner of the entrance hall behind the inquiry desk. Some of the policemen on duty knew some English, but they hardly seemed to be interesting individuals.

May 15

The central feature of the morning was a conducted tour of the interior of the richly decorated YMCA building, with its beautiful reading rooms, swimming pool, and other appurtenances. On the long climb up the tower a large party of youth from a kibbutz was in front of me; and if the view from the top was not absolutely breathtaking, it was indeed a grand experience. One could see not only the old Hebrew University and Hadassah Hospital buildings on isolated Mount Scopus, but also the towers of Ramallah Radio in Jordan, whose English programs I often tune in. A jumble of roofs was all that could be discerned of the Old City, apart from a prominent ruined church or two and a stretch of the Old City walls; but even this was more than could be seen from ground level from certain points of the modern city. No signs of life were visible over the considerable expanse of Jordan territory that spread before me; in contrast, the Jewish city below was busy with traffic everywhere.

Although rather late, I managed to meet my friend at the central police restaurant, where the food was inexpensive and quite as good as the Hazorea fare. Afterwards, he being busy with his own affairs, I went off to the zoo. The Jerusalem Biblical Zoo, as it is called, is for the time being quite a rudimentary affair. Situated on a rocky hillside, it is designed to contain specimens of each animal mentioned in the Bible; inscriptions, quoting the appropriate Biblical verse in Hebrew and English, are fastened to each cage (the cages being rough constructions of wire netting between trees). But, in spite of an impressive diagram suggesting a tremendous collection of animals, I could find very little. I was particularly amused to observe that when

the few monkeys were being fed, the man at the gate had
to desert his post and, ignoring anyone who might come
wandering in, had to lend a hand to his colleague with
the animals. I then tried to get friendly with a small Syrian
bear, but all it did was bite my finger—an instance of
Syrian aggression I might have expected. The mountain
deer, or ibexes, or whatever they were, on the other hand,
were as friendly as the sheep at home.

Back in the city, I utilized the free ticket which I had obtained in the morning to gain admission to the Knesset.
The Israeli parliament is housed in a small, modern, concrete building of agreeable but not striking shape; inside,
its smallness seems remarkable, for it is hardly more than
a big room. From the public gallery one could see little
more than the Speaker's desk, although it was obvious that
the members' seats were arranged in continental horse-
shoe fashion, each member sitting behind his own little
desk. I stayed for only the first few minutes of the first
speech of the evening session, and then went off to another
concert at the YMCA, this time given by the *Kol Yisrael*
radio orchestra and singers. It was an unusual selection of
operatic excerpts, fully worthy of the high musical standards prevailing in this country.

My day was not over even at the end of the concert, for
I had secured from the helpful State Tourist Office an admission ticket to the night broadcasts to the Diaspora.
Before emigrating, I had often listened to the English
transmissions, whose excellent explanatory talks on Israel
affairs undoubtedly had a considerable influence on my decision to come to Israel. I did not plan to stay until one in
the morning, the time of the English broadcast; I could,
however, watch the Yiddish or French transmission,
which were made earlier. I was told to wait in the entrance

hall of the large old mansion which had been converted
into a broadcasting house, and was then led into the studio
for the French broadcast. There was no public gallery as I
had expected, and I was the only visitor; so I simply sat
down at one end of the table on which the microphone
stood, while the lady and gentleman who alternated with
their reading of the news and comments sat at the side.
The informality was amazing; I could have leaned over
and said anything into the microphone had I been bent on
mischief. The announcer sat behind a double glass panel
in one wall, while the controller was stationed at his desk
behind another similar panel in a further wall. The announcer also operated two turntables, and through a play-
back loudspeaker, we could hear the snatches of records
with which he linked his announcements, as well as small
contributions from other studios. Never before had I been
able to enjoy so intimate a contact with broadcasting in
progress—attendance at a B.B.C. studio concert, where the
public is admitted and controlled on a grand scale, is an
entirely different matter. It was midnight by the time I
reached my cot at the police station, after a full and fascinating day.

May 16

This morning I had a good look at the incomplete Con-
vention Center on the approaches to the city: it is certainly
an imposing structure. Turning back to the city, I visited
the Bezalel Museum, which contains a fine assortment of
Jewish works of art, and, timing matters carefully, proceeded to the nearby Jewish Agency and associated buildings. There I attended a showing of a couple of very good
settlement-propaganda films, inspected the enormous, gor-
geously decorated Golden Books which list the names

of donors to Zionist funds, and was shown the room which is a reconstruction of Herzl's Vienna study, with the desk on which he wrote most of his Zionist writings.

The afternoon program comprised a visit to the Greek monastery—a dilapidated but interesting, rambling old place, partly occupied by the Army. Thereafter, with my clarinetist friend, we visited first Mount Zion and then Mount Herzl. I had found out the exact route to Mount Zion from the Tourist Office and, leaving the road, we climbed up the steep, labeled path. Mount Zion's obvious interest lies in the fact that it is a very old Jewish holy place, adjoining the Old City. The only other visitors this evening were an elderly German couple. In going over to the exhibition of sorrowful mementos from the European ghettos after the Nazi holocaust, the man kindly explained a good many points to me in English.

Afterwards, a long bus ride took me to the foot of Mount Herzl, where Theodor Herzl is buried in a circular hilltop garden. The scene, overlooking the Judean hills, with the gracious detached suburbs of Jerusalem nearby, was truly pleasant and impressive in its tranquillity. As the bus ran me back in the dusk, I saw the buildings of Jerusalem gathered together on their ridge—a modern city in the midst of a mountainous, barren wilderness.

May 17

Took leave of my good friend at the police station and caught the early morning train from the rather dingy but roomy old Jerusalem station. The train was quite full, and several people were standing. The ride afforded excellent views down the "Corridor," winding through scenery considerably different from that of the bus route.

In Tel Aviv, I this time included the local zoo in my

tour: a much more lively affair than the quaint Jerusalem attempt. I refrained from going too close to the Syrian bears: they were bigger specimens here in Tel Aviv and looked fiercer, too!

May 24

Back at Hazorea, I was put in charge of clearing up the weeds from the garden around a bungalow built by some old people who gave a lot of money to the kibbutz and settled here. Working unsupervised, I arranged my work hours so that I had a short lunchtime, instead of the usual two-hour midday break. Thus I finished early and took the 4:40 P.M. bus into Haifa to see Walt Disney's *Cinderella*. This was my first visit to an Israeli cinema, and it certainly was an unusual business. The performances are not continuous; tickets are issued for numbered and reserved seats for definite times, just like in the theaters in England. I could get no ticket for the early evening performance but, having chosen a Thursday on which there is a specially late 11:30 bus back to Hazorea, I could wait for the late show. When I eventually got inside, I was astonished to find myself in a room seating about a hundred people. Apparently this is an exceptionally small cinema, tacked on to a main one above. But, even on the small screen, no bigger than the sheet we use on the dining-room wall for our film shows at Hazorea, *Cinderella* was great fun from my point of view. Incidentally, I was pleased to see a "No Smoking" sign in the tiny cinema; presumably this is general here, as in the United States.

May 26

I have finally managed to tackle the unpacking of the suitcase of papers covering the activities of my past life in

England—the last item in my luggage. Who knows how long it will be before this great mass of material, ranging from music programs to tour reports, can be thoroughly sorted out: it will have to be a slow and gradual process, for life is too crowded for a rapid completion of a job like this.

May 31

This being the last day of May, it is suitable to look back over the winter rain. Records of precipitation had been exhibited in the entrance to the dining room, but I never noticed them until they were pointed out to me recently. Soon thereafter they were taken down: the rains are considered over after April. But there was, in fact, a slight thunderstorm in mid-May, concluding the rainy season, no doubt. The records showed that there were three days on which a little rain fell last October, and that the total number of wet days during the winter was forty-seven. They were not wet days in the English sense; here the rain almost always stops after a very few hours, possibly to start again. The amounts recorded ranged from 108 millimeters in January and 96 in February to about 60 in November, December, and April. March and October were minimum months, with less than 15 millimeters. The total was just about 18 inches, which, I am told, is far below the Hazorea average of 24 inches. Hazorea thus has the same annual rainfall as London, with the difference, of course, that instead of being spread over all the year, the rain here falls nearly entirely during the winter half. Also, it is much more definite when it comes, bearing little relation to the light, drizzling rain of Britain over long periods. I am told that the maximum Hazorea rainfall possible is in the neighborhood of 36 inches; so variations are con-

siderable, for the minimum can be around 12. Low rainfall is desirable for us here, since the dense, clayey soil of
the Emek gets waterlogged all too quickly. For other parts
of the country the effects of below-average rainfall are agriculturally serious.

June 1

Our film show was given in the open for the first time
this year; the sheet screen was fixed up on the side of a
truck parked behind the kitchen where the ground slopes
suitably upwards so that an audience can bring its
own chairs or stools and sit in loose rows. The program,
mostly for children, included *The Wizard of Oz*.

June 6

The first grapes of the season replaced plums as dessert
after dinner, but they were not very sweet or even grapey-
flavored. I think it is too early for them yet. I seem to have
been engaged interminably on a vast single-handed job of
clearing the sides of our reservoir-cum-swimming pool of
accumulated weeds, but at last it looks nearly finished. It
is a nice job, as parties of children are always coming along
at different times of the day to have swims in the water
and to watch me work; the adults come in the evening. I
myself, never having learned to swim, am an oddity.

June 10

I missed the festival of first fruits on the playing
field this afternoon. I was detailed to take the sheep to pasture in the Emek stubble fields for half the day. This being
a national holiday, only a quarter-day's work was supposed
to be contributed by everyone (Hazorea apparently never
feels justified in losing revenue to the extent of treating

public holidays as complete) but, as on Independence Day, I get the additional quarter-day "repaid" later on. I gather there was a procession of animals at teatime, and afterwards I inspected the field of operations which was dominated by a decorated stand of hay bundles and boxes, from which speeches had apparently been made.

I have rarely seen a funnier sight in my life than the flock of some four hundred sheep and lambs going down the main road together to or from their happy hunting grounds. With their brown classically curved noses and heads waving up and down and their long ears flapping wildly, the whole gang of them undulates along, spread right across the road, blocking any traffic unfortunate enough to put in an appearance. This picturesque spectacle is most frequently to be enjoyed when they are in a hurry to get home; on the outward journey, in the hot part of the afternoon, they prefer to straggle along the weedy fringe of the road, standing about in groups and often refusing to move on.

June 12

My work was remarkably varied today. I had half a day's gardening, a quarter of a day in the vegetable garden and a quarter of a day with the sheep, relieving the previous shepherd halfway through the afternoon pasture session. While the sheep and I were in the corn field specially sown for them, I saw an odd kind of yellow-green lizard sitting on one of the plant heads. I picked it off—it made no particular attempt to run away—and found it very leathery indeed. It had an absurd prehistoric appearance, as though it were a miniature monster of antediluvian pattern, heavily armored, although only about 4 inches long, with a tail as long again, very thin and waving. It was very good at climbing, and managed to scratch me with its spiky claws, but otherwise was quite harmless, although it opened its mouth immensely wide and made a faint gasping noise suggesting the utmost fury at being interfered with, and looking as though it were shouting, deafeningly. Perhaps it was, according to its own scale of acoustics; I could hardly hear what it said. I suspected it might be a chameleon, but it did not quite agree with the descriptions I had read, which insisted that chameleons had long, coiled-up tongues which shot out to catch insects. However, when I brought it home, wrapped up in my handkerchief, it was diagnosed as a chameleon, after all. Its color-changing abilities seemed a little dubious, but it did turn dirty gray after being shut up in a tin for a time and being stood on some red blotting paper. Perhaps tests under artificial light were hardly fair. The coiled-up tongue, if any, remained coiled up and I never saw it; perhaps no sufficiently attractive insects were observed in the district. The poor wretch seemed quite resigned to my attentions in the end, and made no immediate attempt to run away when I put it outside my hut; later on it disappeared, no doubt with great relief.

Our Youth Group has been down to Elath on the Red Sea for military training, and, having now returned, has arranged a splendid little exhibition of Negev items on top of the grand piano in the dining hall. Various stones and shells, backed by cleverly arranged bottles of colored sands, are very handsome. In the evening, the youngsters gave quite masterly accounts of their experiences, as far as I could gather from my still limited understanding of their Hebrew.

June 18

Another change of work has made me a quite habituated plumpicker all of a sudden. For several mornings now I have been going out with a group on a truck up the wadi to the extensive orchards, which lie in an outlying valley between rough hillsides. Not only do we take breakfast along, and have it picnic fashion, but, at midday, our lunch is brought to us similarly, and we finish our nine hours' work fairly early, at teatime, having, of course, only the briefest lunch interval. I cannot really call this work, although other people do; it is altogether too much like a holiday.

June 21

The great day has arrived! Beth Wilfred, our House of Culture, built as a memorial to Wilfred Israel, who left us the money for it, was opened at a teatime ceremony. A lady from England was the only one of my invitees to turn up, and she was very interested to see the speeches made from the terrace stage which divides the reading room at one end from the museum room at the other. I say "see" rather than "hear" because she could understand hardly any Hebrew. Work on the building had gone on to the last minute; a lamp fixture on the side was still being adjusted a couple of hours before the opening; carpenters and others had worked overtime the evening before. I myself spent the morning helping to transport and arrange empty plum boxes and boards on the stretch of internal roadway outside the dining hall to form trestle tables, designed to cope with the great influx of guests invited. The best episode in this process occurred when one of the boxes fell off a badly loaded tractor-trolley while transporting a consignment across the main road from the orchards, almost to be run over by the afternoon bus to Tiberias! In the evening, my guest and I had supper outside, as it was too hot in the dining hall itself. Although the afternoon attendance was not great, hundreds more came in the evening for the celebration performance. Parties had been invited from various surrounding kibbutzim, and trucks and buses as well as private cars filled up a stretch of the farmyard.

The performance on the terrace stage forming the middle part of Beth Wilfred was an immense success, delighting the audience of about a thousand seated on the sloping lawn in front. I had already seen the rehearsals, so I did not stay for all of Karel Čapek's *Insect Play,* which followed a charming Mozart piece by our splendid choir and tiny orchestra. I went instead, by previous arrangement, to a friend's empty room where I listened on his radio to a magnificent B.B.C. relay of Act III of *The Marriage of Figaro* from Glyndebourne, the unique Southdown opera house so well known to me. Thereafter, I returned to the scene of operations in good time for our own opera, Weber's *Abu Hassan,* which ended at midnight. Bearing comparison with Offenbach, it seems extraordinary that this tuneful singspiel should be so very neglected nowadays. What with the artistic scenery, the fine tenor singing of the hero, our grand choir now acting as chorus, and the splendid efforts of everyone else concerned, including the orchestra of six, the total effect was such as to please, I think, even the performers themselves. Two repeat performances of the whole evening's entertainment which are to follow for the benefit of visitors from other kibbutzim in the district will undoubtedly add appreciable luster to Hazorea's good name.

June 29

There was an interesting excursion by truck to Sarid, the kibbutz just opposite us on the other side of the Emek, this evening. There is no way straight across, apart from a dubious footpath from Mishmar Haemek I have still to discover. One can go part-way towards Haifa and then turn half backwards along the range of hills on the other side; or else start in the opposite direction and then turn across the base of our section of the Emek through Afula. Although quite a few miles longer, this latter way was taken by our three trucks, so we had the best part of an hour's ride. The occasion was the presentation of a play in celebration of the twenty-fifth anniversary of Sarid's founding. Before the play, we saw a fine exhibition arranged in one of the farm buildings. The whole history of Kibbutz Sarid's development, with interesting analyses of its population, land use, and so on, was shown, along with geological specimens of its soil, photographs, and other items. Luckily, I can understand some Hebrew by now, and could read enough of the captions to the various exhibits to appreciate their significance. The audience, said to be three or four thousand, sat on numbered curving rows of bales of straw (no smoking allowed!) which were quite comfortable, each visiting kibbutz group being told the number of its rows. Our own two rows were considerably apart, but both were very far back, and, voice production being bad, we could not hear much. The hillside situation was taken good advantage of for the production, and the scenery and lighting effects were very fine; but, as I was told afterwards, technically speaking the show could not be termed a really good one. Even allowing for personal prejudice and all that, I do not think it challenged the standards set by our own Irish play producer and the head of our building department who produced our opera (in addition to superintending the immense job of building Beth Wilfred—obviously a giant among even the super-men of Hazorea).

I nearly got left behind afterwards, as I could not find the Hazorea trucks in the improvised parking area, and became separated from my party in the crowds. I was rather pleased at the prospect of staying the night in the wood opposite, as Sarid seemed a most interesting place to explore in daylight. We had been able to see almost noth-ing of it in the dusk after arrival. I also wanted to trace my Montevideo friend from the immigrant ship last autumn. At the last minute, however, a Hazorean found me wan-dering about on the road, and guided me to our last truck. Thus I got home after all. I shall certainly have to tackle Sarid on another occasion.

June 30

This afternoon I walked up to Ein Hashofet to see my English friends from the Northwest London branch of the movement who have temporarily settled at our neighbor-ing kibbutz. I had a good, but all too short, time with them, after which I did my best to follow the directions one of the group gave me, and to go directly to Mishmar Haemek, where there were celebrations in progress. The event was the end of the school year at the Mossad, the secondary school which we, among others, share with them. Unfor-tunately, things somehow went wrong with the route, and I found myself following a track down the side of what was evidently the wrong wadi—dry, of course, at this time of year. The path, it is true, swung round toward the Emek all right, and led out to the main road, but instead of being beyond Mishmar Haemek, I found I was nearly halfway back to Hazorea! I made record time along the road after that, and arrived in time for the evening events, at any rate. There was a surprisingly effective little exhibition of handicrafts; I could hardly believe that teenage children could turn out such beautifully finished woodwork, leather-work, and the like. After I had seen this, I witnessed a ceremony such as I had previously seen at Hazorea: apparently the initiation of young members into the local youth group of the movement. The youngsters repeated certain words after the older members, while around them was a ring of flaming torches; it was an impressive ceremony in the balmy night, and against the background of the solemn hills dimly seen. It would, no doubt, be long remembered by the initiates. I did not stay for all of the children's performance, given to a small audience of admiring parents on an open-air stage; but I listened to the young people's choir and orchestra which gave quite good accounts of themselves, and then took to the road and went home.

This was the first occasion on which I had an actual night walk in Israel. The soft, warm night breezes, the familiar rocky hills to one side, and the spreading Emek with the twinkling lights of its scattered settlements on the other, made a pleasingly artistic effect. Over me stretched the starry sky with the Milky Way drawn prominently across it, and I was very impressed.

July 1

I spent the past several days emptying sacks of potatoes into the potato-grading machine which chivvies them through wire grids into collections of different sizes. This afternoon I participated in the grand-finale potato feast, using the machine as table.

After the feast, I decided to have a look at the one and only local shop, since I had never been inside it all the months I have lived nearby. It is only a short way up the road to Yoqneam, a very ordinary general store of the village type, selling large quantities of canned goods and household oddments. As it did not have ice cream, I decided it was of no use to me anyway. As far as I know, it is the only store between the last Haifa suburb and Afula —some twenty miles!

July 3

I have changed over from potato work to viticulture, weeding the rows in the vineyard with the Americans for the first half of each day and picking plums part of the time later. The hoeing is, of course, very dull, but the grapes along the ninety-nine long rows seem to be coming along quite well, although they are far from ripe yet.

In the evening I boarded the bus to Mishmar Haemek to speak to the English teacher there about getting some pen pals, for the pupils of a schoolmaster friend of mine in England. I was somewhat surprised to be taken along free of charge, together with three children who also got on at Hazorea, to enjoy a free ride. There were nearly as many crates of lemonade as there were passengers on the bus, and, on arrival at Mishmar Haemek the driver pulled up at the building where the crates had to be deposited. The only thing the obliging driver did not do was to help carry the crates to their final destination. After obtaining the information I wanted, I had to walk back (there being no bus at that hour); in daylight, the familiar walk was, of course, less impressive than in the dark the other night.

July 4

When I went to supper at about 8:30 as usual, I was surprised to find the dining hall empty and in darkness. Evidently there was some show on, about which I had not heard, I decided to go along to Beth Wilfred and see what was happening there. When I approached, I found the terrace stage full of tables and people sitting at supper there! The head shepherd motioned me to a place opposite him, and for the first time since leaving Europe, I had a perfect European meal of chicken, vegetables, and a double ice cream afterwards. I had no idea what it was about at the time, as no immediate explanation was forthcoming. Afterwards it turned out that it was intended as a special supper for members only (even so the tables overflowed on to the ground at the back of the stage), as the first Beth Wilfred celebrations had included outsiders. This was to be a little private rejoicing for full-fledged Hazoreans only. Mere ordinary people, including guests like me, were supposed to have supper at 6 P.M. I had seen no notice about that, nor been told; but now, covered by the head shepherd's kind invitation, I was accidentally enabled to participate in this most exclusive function. After the remarkable meal, Hazorea's own film in color was shown to those present. Lasting almost half an hour, it consisted of impressions of the life of the kibbutz. The innumerable snippets, showing all sorts of people doing their jobs in the natural surroundings, did not seem to be edited in any particular order, but they were the sort of thing, in total effect, which can make the denizens of sooty cities envy the brilliant, open-air life amid fine scenery which Israel can offer. Our film had, in fact, toured America in the past to help collect funds for Hazorea. One of the

prime scenes in it showed our electrician waving from the
top of one of the electric poles. As it was he who operated
the projector on this occasion, he obligingly turned back
the reel and reran it, to the vast amusement of all his
friends present. Even my sheep appeared in one scene,
but I could not identify the shepherd; the film was made a
year or two before my time.

July 6

Today I actually succeeded in driving a horse and cart!
Having failed to make the donkey go the right way last
winter, I was surprised it worked so well. Steering is remarkably easy, in fact; the slightest pull on the required
rein is enough. Later on, a small boy decided to take over,
and he, used to it from birth, so to speak, did still better.

July 7

The children of our elementary school held an exhibition in one of their classrooms, marking the end of their
school year. I, for one, was delighted with the quality of
their work. Under the project system, by which they learn,
groups cooperate in the production of joint notebooks,
relief maps, etc., and utilize various branches of knowledge
in order to work all round their subject. They turned out
large quantities of material on such themes as "Haifa,"
"China," and "The beginnings of the Jewish State" (going back to Biblical days). The Haifa notebooks contained
diagrams of the port, paragraphs on Mount Carmel, and
so on, and included, in at least one case, a note in English,
written in printed characters. I had been told to expect
this, because the letters are not joined in Hebrew writing,
and consequently Israeli children find it difficult to join letters when writing the Latin alphabet. Beautifully done

handicraft work was in evidence too; by way of contrast there were items of almost futuristic art such as designs in colored paper and scraps of newspaper, cut to shape, and pasted on sheets.

July 10

This evening *Ali Baba* was performed on the stage of Beth Wilfred by our children. They made a fine job of it, acting with a real flair and enthusiasm. These children of the kibbutz are truly intelligent kids, capable of controlling their actions quite responsibly. It says a lot for their teachers.

July 11

I became somewhat yellow this morning and rather black this afternoon: first, I was one of two people operating weed-killer sprays, joined by pipe to the mobile, tractor-drawn pumping machine, and my sprayer was highly leaky. The purpose of the operation was to clear the channel which carries the waste water from the laundry and the showers down into our wadi. After lunch, I had to cover some pipes and fittings with black paint. Splashes of black consequently dotted the yellow stains left by the weed-killer fluid, and at the end of the day, I certainly needed a lengthy visit to the showers to remove, as far as possible, my inadvertent imitation wasp appearance.

July 12

Life is quite varied at present. Apart from a wholesale weed-clearing effort behind the main grain store, my work included digging an irrigation channel for a row of trees leading down towards the main gate. One had to dig a sort of letter *W* formation over the roots in front of each tree, as well as a straight channel at the back, so that the water would run all round the arms of the *W*'s as well as straight along. I think this is almost my favorite job, so I quite enjoyed it, although the water often went the wrong way, or refused altogether to flow round certain *W*'s; it was very much like playing at sand castles on the beach, I thought. But an additional interest consisted in regulating the flow from the tap at the start of the line; that had to be just about right, in order to get the desired results. After an hour or two of weeding, when I went back to have a look at my channeling opposite, the water had more or less successfully reached the last tree.

July 13

Another change of work switched me on to dragging sacks of corn cobs to the edges of a section of our great corn plantation for subsequent collection by tractor and trolley. The pickers were mostly Jerusalem children, junior members of the movement, who are spending a month here in a kind of work camp. They work half the day, thereby supporting themselves during their stay, and have a country holiday for the rest of the time. A similar party of Haifa children is to follow on afterwards. Hazorea seems to be turning itself into quite a holiday camp in the summer. Additional tents and huts are pressed into service, since available accommodations are insufficient. After the picking, one had to empty the sacks and pack the cobs into boxes for market: about thirty to the box. We filled, according to my count, just 450 boxes in the end. Quite a harvest for one day.

In the evening, there was another private phonograph concert in the leading musician's room, but only one or two people attended.

July 14

There was immense activity at Beth Wilfred, both afternoon and evening. The first session, starting soon after midday, comprised the magnetic-tape recording of our *Abu Hassan* by Kol Yisrael, the Israeli broadcasting station, for which it had been recorded for subsequent transmission. I had to go on duty with the sheep at 3 P.M., but I saw a good deal of the preliminary testing. The museum room was linked by wires across the stage with the reading room in which the performance took place. The acoustics are so reverberant that, in the end, several members of the Youth Group had to be invited in, along with blankets and rugs thrown over chairs, to absorb some of the surplus sound.

In the evening, two artistes—Rumanian, I think, although they spoke German here—gave a violin and piano recital. Without reaching any great heights, it was well done. The program included Beethoven's *Kreutzer Sonata* and several smaller pieces. They performed in the doorway of the reading room, leading on to the stage, while the audience was seated partly on the stage and partly on the lawn just below. Acoustically, I think the results could have been improved upon, but the nighttime effect was very pleasant. Behind Beth Wilfred, or the House of Culture as it is officially called, the Hills of Ephraim are dimly seen; the nearest of them, "our" hill, to the left side, is quite prominent even in the faintest moonlight. Behind the sloping lawn stretches our main lawn, with the rose bed and the goldfish pond, complete with water lilies. Some of our bungalow blocks abut onto the garden on each side of the lawn, divided from each other by their own gardens and lawns. The center of our village is really beautifully laid out, and I think Hazorea's version of the "village green" is quite admirable. We have plenty of trees along the edges, too—weeping willows and silver birches, among others. All in all, we have a charming setting for night music, while, of course, its full beauties are revealed only in the brilliance of daylight.

July 15

I felt almost as if I were handling gold dust when I heard that the orange-golden clover seed I was pouring into our new grain pits was worth IL600 to 800 a ton!

July 16

The chief musician borrowed my Benjamin Britten *Young Person's Guide to the Orchestra* record again, in order to play it to the Jerusalem children assembled on the lawn behind the dining hall. From trees over the lawn an electric light is suspended, so that the children can lie there and read in the evenings. I counted an audience of something like fifty children.

July 18

I was introduced to another Irishman today. He knows our play producer (who is still away on his intensive Hebrew course at Nahariya), but came to Israel quite independently. He will stay in Hazorea for a few months at most, as he has equipment on the way to enable him to work as a chiropodist in Tel Aviv. Or else he may become a taxi driver instead! It is rather odd that he should come here, as he is evidently not at all in training as a kibbutznik.

July 20

The third concert of my phonograph records did not turn out very well at Beth Wilfred tonight, because something seems to have deteriorated in the speaker. The records, Mozart's *Exultate Jubilate* motet and the *Piano Concerto* in C, K. 503, along with items from Bliss's film music *Things to Come* and Rawicz and Landauer selections from *Die Fledermaus* and *Der Zigeunerbaron,* were played on the stage, while an audience of about twenty-five listened on the lawn just below. No doubt the acoustics will be much better when we can use the resonant reading room itself (as soon as it gets cooler).

July 21

Quite unbelievably, it rained today—a double shower while I was changing buses in Haifa on my way to Acre —certainly an amazing event in mid-July, although not, I understand, quite unique. Acre is a really remarkable place. I find myself quite unable to describe the old Arab city. I never expected that the Arabs would have built so high and so solidly in stone, as though they were short of space. There seems to be nothing to have prevented the city from spreading inland from the headland on which it is built. There was, I suppose, a tendency to cluster within walls for defense. The busy market street with its open shops; the enormous ruins of the famous castle, the high walls by the sea with walks along the top; the narrow, high houses with crumbling staircases—all looking slightly, but only slightly, ruined—were surpassed in effect by the great mosque with its large courtyard in front, enclosed by almost elegant little houses. After I went up the steps from the street and walked past the fountain in the middle of the tree-lined courtyard, I had to take off my shoes to step into the mosque. It was roomy and bare inside, with garish designs clumsily daubed on the walls, but had nevertheless an atmosphere of its own.

The buses seemed to knock off entirely for an hour or two midday, and thus I was unable to get to the seaside resort of Nahariya a little farther up the coast. In fact, when I eventually got back to Haifa, I was hours late for visiting a friend on Mount Carmel.

July 29

For about a fortnight now I have been sorting thousands of sacks at the sack store—a couple of ex-army huts. Apart from special types, I have had to divide them into suitable piles: small ones, good and bad; large ones ditto; and very good quality, heavy ones, suitable for heavy grain, likewise. The bad ones are afterwards put, nineteen sacks inside a twentieth, and sent for repair.

Today, at last, a new job has cropped up: harvesting carrot seed, or, at any rate, performing the final operations of its harvesting. The valuable clover seed of the other week fades into insignificance beside this: carrot seed is worth something like IL4,000 a ton, I hear! But a large field yields only two to four hundred pounds, I believe—or is it double that?—I am not too sure—so that the yield figures are not really astronomical. The leaves are first cut off from the roots, and gathered in great piles on tarpaulins in the field. They then have to be thrown on to a wide moving belt, driven by a tractor; the belt conveys them to a crushing apparatus at whose other end the seeds come out into sacks. The crushed residue falls out at the bottom, again on to a tarpaulin, so that it does not get mixed up with the earth. Afterwards, we put the residue through the machine again, to make sure none of the very fine seed is wasted. The work proceeded more or less smoothly until one of the tarpaulins became caught in the crushing rollers because we were holding it too far up the moving belt in shaking the final scraps off it. With the aid of my knife and several people crawling into the machine, it took a mere two hours to cut out the pieces and allow work to be resumed. A little while after that, the machine failed to function properly so we gave up in despair and pulled it home to the yard. At first we thought it could be repaired while we were having tea, but we ended up by going home early instead of late. The job will take another day or two to complete.

July 31

This evening a farewell party was given to the Americans. The seminar is now breaking up, at the end of its strenuous six-month course of half-day work and half-day classes in Hebrew, socialism, and Zionism. After a week or two for touring and holidays, its teenage participants are going home to spread the ideas among others in their youth clubs. There was a farewell speech by their leader, who is at present chairman of our weekly general meeting, and the students read Hebrew essays on their experiences here. At least one effort must have been very funny, judging from the laughter it caused among the audience which filled the dining hall, but I did not stay up till the very late end myself.

August 6

My sack sorting has recently been transferred to a new location, adjacent to the dining hall, on which two alumi-

num huts have been erected. They made a good, convenient sack store, only a stone's throw from the grain elevator. Incidentally, brick walls are now being built round
the new grain-cleaning machine and the concrete pits,
along with a new and extended loading platform in front.
Alongside, I swept a stretch of internal road (where we
had our overflow supper on the night of the opening of Beth
Wilfred) as clean as possible, and upon it we spread at least
ten patches of durra—a heavy Mediterranean grain making excellent chicken feed—separated by some of the same
rotten sacks which I had rejected at my sorting operations.
We have grown these different types—some red, some
light gray—for official testing, and they are spread out
in the sun to dry thoroughly before being bagged. One of
my functions is to walk, barefoot, through the durra every
day or two, and turn it over to make sure it all gets completely dry.

Every day now, two of the children bring two goats
and tie them up outside one of the chicken houses nearby. The purpose of this is to enable the goats to eat the
weeds which grow there. And almost as regularly, nearly
every day, I find that one of the goats has escaped during
the morning and is calmly enjoying itself eating the precious durra instead. So another of my duties has become
that of goatcatching and hauling off the absurd animal by
its rope and retying it to its tree or post. If I knew enough
Hebrew, I could tell these children all sorts of things. They
usually get rather muddled up with their goats themselves;
these animals tend to be somewhat bigger than the children concerned, so that they drift across the durra even on
the way to being tied up, let alone afterwards.

August 10

When I went to collect the sheep for pasture this afternoon (as is now again becoming usual for me owing to labor shortage in that department), I found the spraying equipment in full swing in the milking section of the sheepshed. The reason, I found, was surprisingly simple: the sheep were being washed with plain water. At this time of the year they positively walk in a cloud of dust on bare earth. I had to wait quite a long time before the job was finished; they were fastened in their milking stands by the necks as usual, and did not seem to mind the operation at all; probably they liked being cooled off by the water. After it they behaved very well and ate better than usual. I understand they may be washed once a month from now on.

August 13

It always requires two people to get the sheep to move along the first part of their journey in the heat; they hate walking in the sun until they are actually on their pasture ground or at least on the field tracks leading to it from the main road itself. This afternoon, as I was taking the sheep along the road with the aid of one of the shepherds, an American car drew up just ahead. A couple of its inmates produced a tripod and camera and said they wanted to photograph the flock. They wanted the sheep to be in movement, too, so while I proceeded with them they were being filmed. I hope they will be adjudged handsome in Oklahoma or wherever, later on.

At supper time, there was a vaguely pleasant pink fruit mess to eat as dessert. I guessed it was probably the squashy inside of cactus fruits, and so it was. Quite good, especially when suitably refrigerated.

August 14

This evening I was playing records of Mozart's *Prague Symphony* to myself, when a couple of our young boys, not, as far as I knew, noted for being musical, appeared in the doorway and asked if they could listen. They were most interested in my records: I could not fulfill all their requests, which included Russian songs and *Scheherezade* (Rimsky-Korsakov's, not Ravel's, of course), but I was able to produce Haydn's *Toy Symphony* for them.

August 15

Our film shows are now given on a screen which leans up against the stage end of the reading room in the House of Culture, and the audience sits on the lawn, bringing its own stools and chairs if it prefers them to the grass (I do not). Tonight I saw, for the first time, a newsreel produced in Israel; its standard seemed almost equal to foreign ones, I thought, although the sound track seemed dubious. Perhaps our equipment was out of order, though, because the sound track of the film of *La Traviata,* which followed, and which could have been a considerable success, was also deplorably weak. Even so, this show was by far the best we have had for a long time.

August temperatures are usually nearer 90° than 80°; yet I find it possible to work in sun temperatures of 105° and more, as is necessary, without feeling nearly as hot as I used to in a stuffy English heat wave. The continuous western breeze here is both a pleasant surprise and a great asset.

August 22

After lunch I had the unexpected experience of being driven up into the hills to the neighboring kibbutz of Ein Hashofet. It seemed that trouble had developed in their refrigeration machinery, and consequently potatoes we had been storing in their refrigerator house had started to rot. It was necessary now to rebag them and bring a truckload back without delay. When I got there, I found the Hazorea youth group well represented, and we had quite a jolly work session. We got back, after the excellent truck ride downhill (it takes half an hour by road), in time for me to finish sorting the sacks I was engaged upon as usual.

In the evening, I was visited by a member who wished to borrow any books I might have on Victorian England. I have no idea why this German should have become interested in this subject; and unfortunately I could not help him much, because I do not share this particular interest. Still, I was able to lend him Lytton Strachey's *Great Victorians* in the Penguin edition; he thought it might be useful.

August 26

After prolonged negotiations through my kind German lady agent, the Secretary actually saw me in his office concerning my future. I had not anticipated that I would remain merely a guest for almost a full year. The usual practice was to regard six months as a long enough period for being either accepted or rejected as a permanent member. I did not get very far with the Secretary. Using English, instead of the Hebrew he preferred—his own German being, of course, quite unworkable for me—he pointed out that I did not yet know enough Hebrew to participate fully in the life of the kibbutz and that therefore he and his colleagues had not been able to come to any decision about me. I said that I reckoned I had learned perhaps one-quarter of essential Hebrew in nearly one year; that one-half is probably the bare minimum for general comprehension; that it would take quite another year before I should get very far; and that surely they wouldn't let me go on as guest for two years. Laughingly, the Secretary assured me they would make up their minds before that. He asked me what work I wanted to settle in and when I said the sheep, he mentioned that my milking was not quick enough. I replied that I was well aware of that, but what could be expected in the weeks rather than months I had been engaged in milking? He was inclined to admit the force of this point (our moshavnik had had a six months' course, not merely the two months or so during which I had been with the sheep full time). Finally he said that I could make a new approach when I had actually completed my first year, and I had to leave it at that.

August 27

The famous Habimah Theater came to visit Hazorea today, with its production of *Death of a Salesman*. They spent all day fixing up their stage at the track junction, a stone's throw from my hut. Their set was too tall to fit on the stage of our House of Culture. The rows of seats reached back almost to the doorstep of my hut. I went to the beginning of the play but could not make head or tail of the difficult Hebrew involved; so I retired to my room, where I could watch the performers' movements on the stage from my window. Simultaneously, sitting on my bed, I plugged the earphones into my radio and listened to an excellent short-wave transmission from the B.B.C. There was first a radio tour of the Port of London, an item of particular interest to me, as I had done the official Port of London cruise some time before leaving; then a relay of an important concert from the Edinburgh Festival. With my eyes watching Israeli dramatics and my ears in London and Edinburgh, I felt this was a somewhat unique evening with one's personality split between two continents—three, in fact, if one takes into account that the Edinburgh transmission featured the New York Philharmonic Symphony Orchestra.

August 31

I had a typical time sewing up the tops of the sacks filled with corn in the base of the grain elevator. There are apparently enormous quantities of corn to be bagged.

Incidentally, we had our first apples of the season yesterday: one each, carefully handed to us at table. This means that the grape season is well and truly over; they—the grapes, I mean—had been falling off badly in quality for some time now, and were hardly worth eating towards the end. At no point in the season did they really approach the fine flavor of the grapes one usually gets in England, wherever they may come from; they were almost unlimited in quantity though, being the below-grade produce from our own vineyard, and each of us was having a bunch at least once a day.

September 3

Taking the sheep for their afternoon walk, I was astonished to find they refused the field of corn I offered them —the first time they had ever turned up their noses at corn. On returning, I heard they had eaten so much in the morning that they had really overdone it. But that did not stop a few of them from having their usual grab at some of the heifers' food which lies on the ground outside the calf-shed. If the heifers were able to express themselves coherently, their opinion of the sheep would probably be quite interesting to hear.

September 26

Because the sheep insisted on fooling about in some corn that I had told them to stay away from, we were late getting home. Probably frightened by the traffic at dusk, two ewes fell behind and I had to let the main lot run in by themselves while I went back to urge on the stragglers. One was a full-size sheep I rapidly swished on her way, but the other was little "Fatty." Now "Fatty"—no other name is possible—is quite the funniest lamb we have. She is mostly dark-brown or black, with white stripes round her legs, so that it looks as though she were wearing very thick, woolly striped trousers with the stripes horizontal instead of vertical, and inches thick besides. She is so extremely fat that, when she is tired, she can only waddle along at a modest speed and nothing on earth can hurry her up. So I grabbed her by the hair—well, I suppose I am insulting her: wool, then—in the middle of her back, and, to make sure she did not fall behind any more, half dragged her home at her ponderous trot. When she got to the gate of her yard, the poor little thing was so bewildered that she would not go in; so I left her outside while I made sure all the others were safely tucked away. When I went back to look after her I found she was going inside to the farthest corner, looking very nervous indeed. What worrisome lives some little lambs can have!

We had the film *The Red Shoes* this evening. I was particularly glad of this, since I had missed the ending of it when I had previously seen it. As the ending is very important, it was certainly good to see it now—especially sitting on the lawn in front of our House of Culture, under the stars, with our gracious hills behind.

September 28

Today, "Fatty" was last again, but not so very far behind this time: merely the tail member of the gang. And she goes out so gaily too, right up towards the front, poking her little fat nose into everything which suggests food, however distantly, with the utmost energy at first, more like a little pig than a little sheep. Still, with all that fat on, I can quite understand it is a trial to trot home after a four-hour stretch of walking about.

September 30

There was a special distribution of New Year's rations today: not only our usual monthly coffee and sugar, but candy and cookies too. Most surprisingly of all, a tube of cold cream accompanied my quota of comestibles. I am not in the least sure what on earth to do with it. I have heard it is good for sunburn on seaside holidays, but by the time I get my holiday, there will not be much sun. There was a specially good supper too: diced carrots put in a repeat appearance, and there were apple slices which were very nice indeed, after fine servings of meat.

October 1

Great excitement at Hazorea today: the broadcast of our own recorded production of *Abu Hassan,* the Weber operetta, took place at midday. The orchestral accompaniment sounded rather weak, but the singing came over grandly, and everyone was well pleased.

New Year is being celebrated with so many cultural items this week that the whole program has had to be posted on the bulletin board in the dining hall. About half a dozen choice pictures by each of our two artists are on exhibition in the reading room all week; the Sabbath hours of the Eastern antiquities museum with its newly changed display attracted plenty of visitors—when I went to see it, I was handed a set of descriptive notes in English; last night, there was a general party; tonight, the Secretary gave a piano recital—his program of Bach, a late Beethoven sonata, two Debussy preludes, and Milhaud's *Saudades de Brasil* was extremely uncompromising (except for the preludes, which were well known) and most interesting in consequence; on Wednesday, there is to be an evening of dramatic recitations by a noted Israeli artist; Friday is to see a "spoken newspaper" or a political speech. I wonder how many English villages with a total population of 500 could compete with Hazorea in the cultural sphere!

October 2

Our artist, who, in a way, is a full-time practitioner of his avocation, since he is art teacher at the secondary school down the road, was doing his turn of duty waiting at the tables today. The dining room in which he worked is decorated with its own small, but pleasantly designed, murals between the windows. One could draw a lot of morals about this personal admixture of art and life. One could also complain that it was inadvisable. But the artist himself has an irrepressibly happy nature and shows no sign of dissatisfaction. Meanwhile, I think, we need yet another term with which to characterize our classless society here: artistic democracy.

October 3

A scorpion stung me this afternoon. It was a most surprising incident. We had just brought back three hundred sacks from our local sack-repairer at Yoqneam, and as I was putting them away in our nice new sack store, I must have touched the scorpion. It ran away so fast that I barely managed to catch sight of it before it disappeared behind the pile; I reckoned it was more than an inch in size. I could not blame the scorpion, as it was obviously terribly frightened; but it left my thumb in a fearful state, so I trotted off to the clinic, where I found the doctor having tea. He obligingly dug up the nurse, who stuck an injection in my arm on his instructions, in order to neutralize some of the sting. It did nothing of the sort, and although my thumb was bandaged up, it remained in a violent condition for sixteen hours, after which the sting quite suddenly faded away.

October 7

The lady superelocutionist, whose visit had been postponed, gave her performance after supper. I did not stay for all of it, as I could not make much of her literary Hebrew, but the sleepwalking scene from Macbeth seemed very impressively done.

In the afternoon we actually had our first autumn rain; not much—a gentle start this time. Perhaps it was like this last October as well, when I was still touring Europe on the way here.

October 9

Jumping off a small step outside the dining hall, where I was emptying a little grain rubbish into the garbage cans, I fell right over on one ankle and twisted it badly. The pain subsided afterwards so that I was able to continue work.

October 11

My ankle, having swollen up very much, refused to yield to cold-poultice treatment; this morning I was told to leave work and keep the strained ankle up on the bed for a day or two till it gets better.

October 14

The ankle is still as bad as ever. The doctor saw it and ordered a visit to the main workers' clinic in Haifa for X ray. I duly took an early bus to town. My bus tickets for the round trip, money for expenses, and documents for the clinic had all been provided before I left. I spent the whole morning waiting around for the X ray and all that. When I was finally fixed up, with the leg bandaged to a plaster support so as to keep it from bending at the ankle, I had an hour's wait for the next bus home. I used the time to see the Chagall exhibition at Haifa Town Hall, hobbling around laboriously. The exhibition was a colossal success from my point of view. Then back, to stick to my bed for a week.

October 21

There was a Sukkot (tabernacles) party which I had to miss because of my ankle. My Greek neighbor and friend told me it was an impressive affair. I shall have to make sure of attending it next year. There was a very comical play about a tractor breaking down (I could hear some of the laughter far off through my window, so it must really have been funny); then folk dancing went on until about 1:30 in the morning, I gather. I imagine this harvest festival in the autumn is the liveliest show in the year after the terrific Purim games in the spring.

October 23

After an additional two days' delay, owing to lack of facilities on the closing days of Sukkot, I was taken in a member's car to the Haifa clinic. Although I was passed as all right, I was brought home by taxi by another member who also attended the clinic. An ordinary bandage, which enabled me to walk while giving additional support to the ankle, replaced the plaster affair.

According to the grain-handling chief, who kindly came to see me while I was incapacitated and whose wife is the chief nurse, I had actually broken some bone or other, although I heard nothing crack at the time. It could only have been a small connecting one, I should think, as it is only a fortnight altogether since the accident occurred. Actually, I had a wonderful holiday in my room, was able to devise a new dial-marking arrangement for my radio, read several books, record a good deal of data about my past English activities based on my old notebooks, and so on. The meals were brought to me all the time, the special food for ill people, including chicken, puddings, and other items. When I said that this special treatment was unnecessary, as there was nothing wrong with my insides, they replied that it was the usual thing: it helped to relieve the dullness of life when one was stuck in one's room. Also, relays of people are regularly recruited to look after the sick; one day I was attended by my own carpenter-Hebrew teacher!

October 25

After lunch, I was taken from my sack sorting to assisting with an infernal arrangement of pump-and-pipes in spraying the feeding troughs in the sheepshed. Spraying water is, of course, a delightful pastime, but neither my chief nor I could say that we managed to get things thoroughly clean. However, I trust the animals were reasonably satisfied when they came home from pasture and saw what we had done for them. The shepherds made no comment, which may have been just as well.

October 30

An evening excursion to the Chagall exhibition in Haifa was arranged; thus I was able to go for the second time. As an official expedition, it was paid for from the cultural budget, at party rate, and about eighty of us took advantage of these arrangements. Bus travel was provided, instead of the usual truck, so it was quite a luxurious affair. It became even more so on the way home, when the bus stopped at a Haifa cafe and we were all provided with ice cream, presumably this too out of the cultural budget, which must be in quite a good shape at present.

October 31

Well, my first year in the land ends today. What summing up is possible—or desirable? Almost none, I feel, can be really appropriate; and the dangers of generalizing are difficult to avoid. Everyone would sum up differently; but no one would have a sufficient basis to do so adequately, for a year is not long enough to get deeply into the spirit of the kibbutz or to grasp the realities of the land and the language.

This much, however, can certainly be said in conclusion. Kibbutz life is a form of existence past pioneers in other countries never experienced on anything more than an experimental and transitional scale, and, except for a few religious groups, without any planned organization. Today, only in Israel can one experience the vigorous constructiveness of pioneering known to those who rolled the American frontier westwards in the last century. Only in Israel can one participate in a large-scale experiment in collective living the like of which the world has not yet known. In the Israeli kibbutz it will shortly be the turn of the third generation to demonstrate to the rest of mankind that the Jewish people, returning to their ancient homeland, have turned the prophetic principles of the Bible into a solid reality of modern times. No Communist commune attempts to attain the voluntary democracy, the total equality, the brotherly pooling of lives in unified effort, and the sharing of achievement which are the basis of the kibbutz.

I know that from now on this is the way of life for me, and I am sure it could be for many others if only they came to try it and thus conquer their natural but unnecessary fear of the unknown.

Appendices

1. The Arithmetic of the Kibbutz

Statistical appendices are rarely read, except by specialists. In some cases, perhaps, their neglect by the reader is justified, in that they add little to his comprehension of the subject. But this can hardly be said to be the case where the kibbutzim are concerned. From a qualitative description, it is very easy to get a mistaken impression of the quantitative aspects of the kibbutz. One may come to regard the kibbutzim as the dominant feature in Israeli life, which (perhaps unfortunately) would be an exaggeration. Or, one may conclude the opposite —that the kibbutz is an interesting but insignificant element in modern Israel—and again one would be quite wrong. A few basic figures in the arithmetic of the kibbutz can indicate what the true situation is.

Take for a start the figures showing the growth of the kibbutzim from 1941 to 1961, and the percentage they comprised of the Jewish population of Israel:

TABLE 1

Year	Number of Kibbutzim	Kibbutz Population	Jewish Population	Per Cent
1914		180	85,000	0.2
1922		735	83,790	0.9
1927		3,909	148,000	2.6
1931		4,391	174,610	2.5
1936		16,444	370,990	4.4
1941	83	27,738	474,183	5.85
1947		47,408	630,019	7.5
1951	213	67,618	1,404,392	4.7
1959		81,946	1,858,841	4.4
1961	223	85,000*	1,950,000*	4.4*

* Estimates.

This is, however, only one aspect of the matter. It is more revealing to look at the figures for one particular year in some detail. 1959 is the most recent year for which full statistics are available. In that year the kibbutz population was 81,946 and the total rural population (not including the Arab minority) was 321,126; i.e., the kibbutz population was just over 25 per cent of the total rural Jewish population. But of the kibbutz population, only 77,890 persons were to be found at home; the other 4,056 were working outside the settlement, filling all manner of posts from agricultural and technical services at home and abroad to acting as Members of Parliament.

The distribution between the various kibbutz movements in 1959 was as follows:

TABLE 2

Federation	Population	Per Cent
Ihud Hakvutzot Vehakibbutzim	25,046	30.5
Hakibbutz Haartzi	27,690	33.8
Hakibbutz Hameuhad	23,265	28.4
Haoved Hatzioni	1,173	1.4
Hapoel Hamizrachi	3,335	4.1
Agudat Israel	561	0.7
Independent (nonfederated)	876	1.1
Total	81,946*	100.0

* It may be added that of the population of 81,946, 43,913 were men, and 38,033 women, or 53.5 and 46.5 per cent, respectively.

Nearly half the kibbutz population are actual members, while most of the rest are children; there are, of course, also some candidates for membership, aged parents of members and so on.

There was a total increase of kibbutz population in the years 1948–1959, of 34,539. Of this, 21,715 was due to natural increase, and 12,824 represents the net addition of newcomers after deduction of those who have left.

The table which follows shows what happened to the new-comers to the kibbutzim during the four years from October 1, 1956, to October 1, 1960. Roughly two-thirds of them remained, and this proportion may be taken as an indication of the particular kind of human material involved. The "material" in this instance was, for the most part, new immigrants from Eastern Europe, and urban young Israelis who joined kibbutzim in response to the "Town to Country" movement. Only to a very small extent did this human "material" contain kibbutzic idealists. Yet, on the whole, two-thirds of them decided to remain within the kibbutz.

TABLE 3

Federation	Entered	Left	Remained	Per Cent Remaining
Ihud Hakvutzot Vehakibbutzim	3,338	905	2,433	73
Hakibbutz Haartzi	3,331	918	2,413	72
Hakibbutz Hameuhad	3,855	1,708	2,147	56
Haoved Hatzioni	277	75	202	73
The religious kibbutzim	388	92	296	76
The independent kibbutzim	198	23	175	88
Total	11,387	3,721	7,666	67

Turning now to the comparative weight of the kibbutz movement in Israeli production, we find that, in 1937, the kibbutzim were responsible for 11.1 per cent of the total Jewish agricultural production in the country; in 1949 for 29.5 per cent; in 1954 for 30 per cent; and in 1958 for 28 per cent (the percentages are based on market values). That is to say, the kibbutz population has produced more than its proportionate share in the country's food and other cultivated items. This was due to the high degree of mechanization and technical skill available on the large, well-planned, and fully coordinated kibbutz farms.

In 1959 the kibbutzim were producing the following percentages in Jewish agricultural output:

	Per Cent		Per Cent
Wheat	66	Citrus fruit for export	6.5
Barley	53	Grapes	20
Corn	56	Bananas	87
Hay	55	Apples and other fruits	48
Cotton	31	Milk	28
Potatoes	35	Eggs	22
Other Vegetables	13	Beef	17

The percentages vary widely, because in some cases production has long been organized by private farming enterprise; in others the kibbutzim have only recently entered the branch in question.

In industry the kibbutzim have not as yet made their weight felt, although their economic future may lie largely in it. Meanwhile, they have already made a good start. In 1951, the kibbutzim produced 3.1 per cent of all Israeli industrial output (again based on market values); in 1955, 4.2 per cent, and in 1959, 5.8 per cent. In the latter year they were producing 23 per cent of the value of all the furniture and wood products then being made in Israel. This is the chief kibbutz industry at present. Production of other items rarely exceeds 5 per cent of the national total, and in many cases is only 1 or 2 per cent or less. The range of products, from shoes to electrical goods, from clothing to chemical products, is very wide, and, as in agriculture, percentages are likely to rise. The kibbutzim are already the most heavily industrialized sector of the Israeli population (in relation to number of people involved), a most surprising fact considering that they are often situated at remote frontier points.

Their progressive industrialization is shown by the following table:

TABLE 4

Year	Persons Employed in Kibbutz Industry	Total Number Employed in All Israeli Industry	Per Cent
1945	1,576	66,000	2.4
1951	3,900	119,000	3.3
1959	10,757	149,400	7.2

Finally, a few general figures regarding the kibbutzim. They maintain two publishing houses with a vigorous, nationwide program. They are essential supports to two daily newspapers. They publish three sizable weeklies and three large and serious quarterlies. They have a symphony orchestra. They run three national choirs and eighty-eight smaller local ones, and have some eighty-five active drama groups. In kibbutzim are located ten large museums and about one hundred small local archaeological collections.

The kibbutzim, then, do not dominate the Israeli world, but they constitute a sizable segment of it, integrated at innumerable points into the Israeli national scene. Their growth is slow but sure. Their present position can be maintained on the basis of their natural increase, estimated at about $2\frac{1}{2}$ per cent per annum, but for expansion they depend upon outside recruitment which alone can bring their marvelous enterprise to full fruition in our time.

2. The Kibbutzim of Israel, 1961

In the following list, approximately the latitude of the north-
eastern corner if the Gaza Strip has been taken as the division
between the Coast Plain and the "South," and the latitude of
Beersheba as that between the South and the Negev. There
is certainly room for disagreement here, although it is felt
that the arrangement adopted has climatic and other justifi-
cations, give or take a few miles here and there. The Huleh
(or Hula) Valley has been separated from the rest of Upper
Galilee, in view of its very much hotter climate—it is, of
course, the Upper Jordan Valley, now minus Lake Huleh and
its swamps, which have been drained and converted into rich
fields. But it should be appreciated that the mountain kibbutzim above have fields and fishponds in the fertile valley below,
alongside those of the kibbutzim actually situated in the valley
itself, in order to assist their economies. The "Jordan Valley"
of the list includes the kibbutzim on the shores of the Sea of
Galilee as well as those in the narrow part of the valley southwards and those on the higher terraces of the Jordan depression
still farther south constituting the Beit Shan Valley at the
junction with the Emek Jezreel, known simply as "The Emek."
"Galilee Coast" has been coined as a name for the northern
part of the Coast Plain extending from Haifa to the Lebanese
frontier, and has been stretched to include the whole of
Emek Zebulun, which itself runs from the northern end of the
Emek to Acre and the mountains behind. Some kibbutzim in it
are therefore several miles inland from the sea. The Menashe

(Manasseh) Hills, sometimes erroneously called the Hills of Ephraim, can be regarded as a southeasterly extension of Mount Carmel, separating the Emek from the Coast Plain. The Jerusalem Hills are, of course, that part of the Judean Mountains lying in the Jerusalem "Corridor," including the foothills rising from the Coast Plain.

Name of Kibbutz	Year Founded	Federation	Location
Afeq	1939	Meuhad	Galilee Coast
Afiqim	1932	Ihud	Jordan Valley
Alonim	1938	Meuhad	Lower Galilee
Alumot	1941	Ihud	Lower Galilee
Amiad	1946	Ihud	Upper Galilee
Amir	1939	Artzi	Huleh Valley
Ashdot Yaaqov A	1933	Ihud	Jordan Valley
Ashdot Yaaqov B	1933	Meuhad	Jordan Valley
Ayelet Hasha-har	1918	Ihud	Upper Galilee
Bahan	1953	Ihud	Coast Plain
Bar Am	1949	Artzi	Upper Galilee
Barqayi	1949	Artzi	Coast Plain
Beeri	1946	Meuhad	South*
Beerot Yitzhaq	1948	Hapoel Hamiz-rahi	Coast Plain
Beit Alfa	1922	Artzi	Jezreel Valley
Beit Guvrin	1949	Meuhad	Coast Plain
Beit Haemeq	1949	Ihud	Galilee Coast
Beit Hashitta	1935	Meuhad	Jezreel Valley
Beit Nir	1955	Artzi	Coast Plain
Beit Oren	1939	Meuhad	Mount Carmel
Beit Qama	1949	Artzi	South
Beit Qeshet	1944	Meuhad	Lower Galilee
Beit Zera	1927	Artzi	Jordan Valley
Bror Hayil	1948	Ihud	South
Dafna	1939	Meuhad	Huleh Valley
Dalia	1939	Artzi	Menashe Hills†
Dan	1939	Artzi	Huleh Valley
Degania A	1910	Ihud	Jordan Valley
Degania B	1920	Ihud	Jordan Valley
Dorot	1941	Ihud	South

* South: The area to the east of the Gaza Strip.
† Menashe Hills: The mountain range south of the Carmel, separating the Northern Sharon in the west from Jezreel Valley in the east.

Name of Kibbutz	Year Founded	Federation	Location
Dovrat	1946	Ihud	Lower Galilee
Dvir (also called Dvira)	1951	Artzi	South
Einat	1925	Ihud	Coast Plain
Ein Carmel	1947	Meuhad	Coast Plain
Ein Dor	1948	Artzi	Lower Galilee
Ein Gedi	1953	Ihud	Dead Sea Coast
Ein Gev	1937	Ihud	Jordan Valley
Ein Hahoresh	1931	Artzi	Coast Plain
Ein Hamifratz	1938	Artzi	Galilee Coast
Ein Hanatziv	1946	Hapoel Hamiz-rahi	Jordan Valley
Ein Hashlosha	1950	Haoved Hatzioni	South
Ein Hashofet	1937	Artzi	Menashe Hills
Ein Harod A	1921	Meuhad	Jezreel Valley
Ein Harod B	1921	Ihud	Jezreel Valley
Ein Shemer	1927	Artzi	Coast Plain
Ein Tzurim	1949	Hapoel Hamiz-rahi	Coast Plain
Elon	1938	Artzi	Western Galilee
Erez	1949	Ihud	South
Even Yitzhaq (also called Gal Eid	1945	Ihud	Menashe Hills
Evron	1945	Artzi	Galilee Coast
Eyal	1949	Meuhad	Coast Plain
Gaash	1951	Artzi	Coast Plain
Gaaton	1948	Artzi	Western Galilee
Gadot	1949	Meuhad	Huleh Valley
Galon	1946	Artzi	Coast Plain
Gan Shmuel	1913	Artzi	Coast Plain
Gat	1942	Artzi	Coast Plain
Gazit	1948	Artzi	Lower Galilee
Gesher	1939	Meuhad	Jordan Valley
Gesher Haziv	1949	Ihud	Galilee Coast
Geva	1921	Ihud	Jezreel Valley
Gevar Am	1942	Meuhad	Coast Plain

Name of Kibbutz	Year Founded	Federation	Location
Gezer (also called Hadasa)	1945	Ihud	Coast Plain
Ginnegar	1922	Ihud	Jezreel Valley
Ginnosar	1937	Meuhad	Jordan Valley
Givat Brenner	1928	Meuhad	Coast Plain
Givat Haim A	1932	Meuhad	Coast Plain
Givat Haim B	1932	Ihud	Coast Plain
Givat Hashlosha	1925	Meuhad	Coast Plain
Givat Oz	1949	Artzi	Jezreel Valley
Glil Yam	1943	Meuhad	Coast Plain
Gonen	1951	Ihud	Huleh Valley
Gvat	1926	Meuhad	Jezreel Valley
Gvim	1947	Ihud	South
Gvulot	1943	Artzi	Western Negev
Hafetz Haim	1944	Agudat Israel	Coast Plain
Hagoshrim	1948	Meuhad	Huleh Valley
Hahotrim	1948	Meuhad	Coast Plain
Haogen	1946	Artzi	Coast Plain
Haon	1949	Ihud	Jordan Valley
Hamaapil	1945	Artzi	Coast Plain
Hamadiya	1942	Ihud	Lower Galilee
Hanitz	1938	Ihud	Western Galilee
Harel	1948	Artzi	Jerusalem Hills
Hasollelim	1949	Haoved Hatzioni	Lower Galilee
Hatzerim	1946	Artzi	South
Hatzor	1946	Ihud	Coast Plain
Hazorea	1936	Artzi	Jezreel Valley
Heftziba	1922	Meuhad	Jezreel Valley
Horshim	1955	Artzi	Coast Plain
Hulata	1937	Meuhad	Huleh Valley
Hulda	1930	Ihud	Coast Plain
Huqoq	1945	Meuhad	Lower Galilee
Idmit	1958	Artzi	Western Galilee
Kabri	1949	Meuhad	Galilee Coast

Name of Kibbutz	Year Founded	Federation	Location
Karmiya	1950	Artzi	Coast Plain
Kfar Aza	1951	Ihud	South
Kfar Blum	1943	Ihud	Huleh Valley
Kfar Giladi	1916	Ihud	Upper Galilee
Kfar Glikson	1939	Haoved Hatzioni	Menashe Hills
Kfar Hahoresh	1933	Ihud	Lower Galilee
Kfar Hamak-kabi	1936	Ihud	Galilee Coast
Kfar Hanasi	1948	Ihud	Upper Galilee
Kfar Masaryk	1938	Artzi	Galilee Coast
Kfar Menahem	1937	Artzi	Coast Plain
Kfar Ruppin	1938	Ihud	Jordan Valley
Kfar Szold	1942	Meuhad	Huleh Valley
Kinneret	1908*	Ihud	Jordan Valley
Kissufim	1951	Meuhad	South
Lahav	1952	Artzi	South
Lavi	1949	Hapoel Hamiz-rahi	Lower Galilee
Lehavot Haba-shan	1945	Artzi	Huleh Valley
Lehavot Ha-viva	1949	Artzi	Coast Plain
Lohmei Ha-getaot	1949	Meuhad	Galilee Coast
Maabarot	1933	Artzi	Coast Plain
Maagan	1949	Ihud	Jordan Valley
Maagan Mi-khael	1949	Meuhad	Coast Plain
Maale Haha-misha	1938	Ihud	Jerusalem Hills
Maanit	1942	Artzi	Coast Plain
Maayan Ba-rukh	1947	Ihud	Huleh Valley

* Although it preceded the founding of Degania, the original commune at Kenneret was transferred to adjacent Degania, which thus became the first continuous kibbutz.

Name of Kibbutz	Year Founded	Federation	Location
Maayan Tziv	1938	Ihud	Mount Carmel
Magal	1953	Ihud	Coast Plain
Magen	1949	Artzi	South
Mahanayim	1939	Meuhad	Upper Galilee
Malkiya	1949	Meuhad	Upper Galilee
Manara (also called Galilim or Ramim)	1943	Meuhad	Upper Galilee
Masada	1937	Ihud	Jordan Valley
Mashabei Sade	1949	Meuhad	Northern Negev
Matsuba	1940	Ihud	Western Galilee
Matzor	1953	Artzi	Coast Plain
Mefalsim	1949	Ihud	South
Megiddo	1949	Artzi	Jezreel Valley
Meoz Hayim	1937	Meuhad	Jordan Valley
Merhavia	1910	Artzi	Jezreel Valley
Mesillot	1938	Artzi	Jezreel Valley
Mifratz Elath	1961	Meuhad	Red Sea Coast
Misgav Am	1945	Meuhad	Upper Galilee
Mishmar David	1948	Ihud	Coast Plain
Mishmar Haemeq	1926	Artzi	Jezreel Valley
Mishmar Hanegev	1946	Meuhad	South
Mishmar Hasharon	1933	Ihud	Coast Plain
Mishmarot	1933	Ihud	Coast Plain
Mizra	1923	Artzi	Jezreel Valley
Naan	1930	Meuhad	Coast Plain
Nahal Oz	1951	Ihud	South
Nahsholim	1948	Meuhad	Coast Plain
Nahshon	1950	Artzi	Jerusalem Hills
Nahshonim	1949	Artzi	Coast Plain
Negba	1939	Artzi	Coast Plain
Neot Mordekhai	1946	Independent	Huleh Valley

Name of Kibbutz	Year Founded	Federation	Location
Netiv Hala-med-he	1949	Meuhad	Jerusalem Hills
Netzer Sereni	1948	Ihud	Coast Plain
Neve Etan	1938	Ihud	Jordan Valley
Neve Or	1949	Meuhad	Jordan Valley
Neve Yam	1939	Ihud	Coast Plain
Nir Am	1943	Ihud	South
Nir David (also called Tel Amal)	1936	Artzi	Jezreel Valley
Nir Eliahu	1950	Ihud	Coast Plain
Nirim	1949	Artzi	South
Nir Oz	1955	Artzi	South
Nir Yitzhaq	1949	Artzi	South
Nitzanim	1943	Haoved Hatzioni	Coast Plain
Or Haner	1957	Ihud	South
Palmahim	1949	Meuhad	Coast Plain
Parod (also called Gar-dosh)	1949	Meuhad	Upper Galilee
Qedma	1946	Meuhad	Coast Plain
Qiriat Anavim	1920	Ihud	Jerusalem Hills
Ramat David	1926	Ihud	Jezreel Valley
Ramat Hako-vesh	1932	Meuhad	Coast Plain
Ramat Hasho-fet	1941	Artzi	Menashe Hills
Ramat Rahel	1926	Ihud	Jerusalem Hills
Ramat Yoha-nan	1932	Ihud	Galilee Coast
Ramot Mena-she	1948	Artzi	Menashe Hills
Regavim	1948	Meuhad	Menashe Hills
Revadim	1948	Artzi	Coast Plain
Revivim	1943	Meuhad	Northern Negev

Name of Kibbutz	Year Founded	Federation	Location
Reshafim	1948	Artzi	Jordan Valley
Reiim	1949	Meuhad	South
Rosh Haniqra	1949	Ihud	Western Galilee
Ruhama	1944	Artzi	South
Saad	1947	Hapoel Hamiz-rahi	South
Saar	1948	Artzi	Galilee Coast
Sarid	1926	Artzi	Jezreel Valley
Sasa	1949	Artzi	Upper Galilee
Schiller (also called Gan Shlomo)	1927	Ihud	Coast Plain
Sde Boqer	1952	Independent	Northern Negev
Sde Eliahu	1939	Hapoel Hamiz-rahi	Jordan Valley
Sde Nahum	1937	Meuhad	Jezreel Valley
Sde Nehemia (also called Huliot)	1940	Ihud	Huleh Valley
Sde Yoav	1956	Artzi	Coast Plain
Sdot Yam	1940	Meuhad	Coast Plain
Shaalvim	1951	Agudat Israel	Coast Plain
Shaar Haama-qim	1935	Artzi	Jezreel Valley
Shaar Hagolan	1937	Artzi	Jordan Valley
Shamir	1944	Artzi	Huleh Valley
Shamrat	1948	Artzi	Galilee Coast
Shefayim	1935	Meuhad	Coast Plain
Shluhot	1948	Hapoel Hamiz-rahi	Jordan Valley
Shuval	1946	Artzi	South
Tel Qatzir	1949	Ihud	Jordan Valley
Tel Yitzhaq	1938	Haoved Hatzioni	Coast Plain
Tel Yosef	1921	Ihud	Jezreel Valley
Tirat Tzvi	1937	Hapoel Hamiz-rahi	Jordan Valley
Tzeelim	1947	Ihud	South

Name of Kibbutz	Year Founded	Federation	Location
Tzora	1948	Ihud	Jerusalem Hills
Tzova	1948	Meuhad	Jerusalem Hills
Urim	1946	Ihud	South
Usha	1936	Ihud	Galilee Coast
Yad Hana A	1950	Independent	Coast Plain
Yad Hana B	1954	Meuhad	Coast Plain
Yad Morde-khai	1943	Artzi	Coast Plain
Yagur	1922	Meuhad	Galilee Coast
Yaqum	1947	Artzi	Coast Plain
Yasur	1949	Artzi	Galilee Coast
Yavne	1941	Hapoel Hamiz-rahi	Coast Plain
Yehiam	1946	Artzi	Western Galilee
Yezreel	1948	Ihud	Jezreel Valley
Yifat	1936	Ihud	Jezreel Valley
Yiftah	1948	Ihud	Upper Galilee
Yiron	1949	Meuhad	Upper Galilee
Yotvata	1951	Ihud	Southern Negev
Yuvalim (also called Mitz-pei Yodfat)	1960	Independent	Lower Galilee
Ziqim	1949	Artzi	Coast Plain